"I've been a huge fan of JIM HAROLD'S CAMPFIRE since the very first episode in April 2009. For me, it's not only great entertainment—the CAMPFIRE podcast is also incredibly inspiring to me as a storyteller. But as much as I enjoy listening to Jim's program on my iPod and hearing weird tales around a real-life campfire, I have to say that ghost-story books are still my favorite way to get spooked. I'm so pleased that I can savor the best CAMPFIRE stories all over again with a blanket and flashlight, just like I did when I was a child."

—Camille DeAngelis, author of *Mary Modern* and *Petty Magic*

"A wonderful collection of stories. Jim Harold's ability to combine the strange and uncanny with everyday life is an art form in itself and sets off perfectly the unusual tales of his correspondents. Long may he continue to collect and enchant. A worthy addition to any library."

—Dr. Bob Curran, folklorist and author of *Vampires* and *Man-Made Monsters*

Jim Harold's

CAMPFIRE
True Ghost Stories

JIM HAROLD

New Page Books
A division of The Career Press, Inc.
Pompton Plains, N.J.

JIM HAROLD'S CAMPFIRE: TRUE GHOST STORIES
EDITED AND TYPESET BY KARA KUMPEL
Cover design by Wes Youssi/M80 Design
Printed in the U.S.A.

To order this title, please call toll-free 1-800-CAREER-1 (NJ and Canada: 201-848-0310) to order using VISA or MasterCard, or for further information on books from Career Press.

The Career Press, Inc.
220 West Parkway, Unit 12
Pompton Plains, NJ 07444
www.careerpress.com
www.newpagebooks.com

Library of Congress Cataloging-in-Publication Data

Harold, Jim.
    Jim Harold's campfire : true ghost stories / by Jim Harold.
        p. cm.
    Includes bibliographical references and index.
    ISBN 978-1-60163-194-7 -- ISBN 978-1-60163-632-4 (ebook)
1. Ghosts. I. Title. II. Title: Campfire.

BF1461.H34 2011
133.1--dc23
                                                            2011026925

To Dar, Cass, & Nat:
You are the lights of my life. I love you all so much!

To Mom, Dad, & John:
No you = no Jim Harold. Love always.

To Al: Thanks for everything.

To Rich: Thanks for being my best friend.

Acknowledgments

To Annie Wilder & Jeff Belanger, without whom you would not be reading this book.

Thanks Annie & Jeff!

To Maddy,

Thanks for all of your help!

To Michael, Adam, and the whole team at New Page Books, your professionalism and enthusiasm are un-matched. Thanks!

Contents

Part IV: Something out of This World

Introduction

Somehow people feel comfortable telling me their spooky stories—a demon who appears in a Lava Lamp during a Ouija board session, a haunted hospital where a long-dead nurse brings a patient a cup of tea, or a haunted bed that shakes at night for no reason! I often ask myself this question: *As a professional family man, how did I end up getting involved in all of this strangeness with these people and their weird tales?*

Well, I think it was fate that I would end up being involved in some way with the paranormal. As a child, I was always drawn to stories of the strange, the weird, and the inexplicable. Thankfully, I've never outgrown it.

Whether it was life after death, ghosts, Bigfoot, or UFOs, I've always been fascinated with the unknown. In 2005, I married my love of broadcasting with this obsession and started THE PARANORMAL PODCAST. For those not indoctrinated, *podcast* is a fancy term for an Internet radio show. You can find my programs at jimharold.com.

Quite unexpectedly, the show has become one of the most popular programs of its type in the world. I have interviewed best-selling authors, experts, and researchers on their theories on our mysterious world. I've learned a lot from them, and yet I have even more questions about the paranormal than I had before I started. Doing THE PARANORMAL PODCAST has always been fascinating to me, but I knew there was something missing in my programs— stories of the average person and their tales of high strangeness.

To fill the void, while continuing the main show, I added a companion production called JIM HAROLD'S CAMPFIRE that focuses on just that—everyday people and their supernatural stories. I have spoken to listeners from every corner of the globe, including Ireland, Japan, Australia, Norway, the United Kingdom, and the United States. It is incredible to me that there is such a universality to this subject; so many common themes and yet so many diverse experiences.

To me, it speaks to the reality of paranormal phenomena. The skeptic would say that, many times, stories of the paranormal are outright hoaxes, the mistaken perceptions of good people seeing what they want to see, or the ramblings of the mentally unstable. I will concede the point that many stories, in fact, do fall into these categories. However, even if a small percentage of these stories are real, scientifically inexplicable phenomena, then we have something. In talking to my CAMPFIRE listeners, I have come to believe that the vast majority, if not all, are telling what they believe to be the truth. I would submit that some of them have experienced just what they have perceived—a real brush with the supernatural.

When I named the show, I just thought *campfire* was a catchy moniker. I was wrong. My listeners have made it much more than that—an electronic version of the old family campfire where we sit around in a comfortable setting and tell spooky stories. It really has brought me and the audience closer together, and the program has had an impact on people that I never anticipated. Many listeners have told me that the program serves as kind of a paranormal support group. I give no psychological advice nor claim any expertise in that field whatsoever, but I do think that it is therapeutic for experiencers to know that others from around the globe have also seen things they cannot explain by mere logic. Via this shared electronic campfire, we realize that we are not alone and that most people have had strange experiences that they cannot begin to explain by rational means.

The chapters in this book are real stories from my listeners. I hope you enjoy these stories as much as I have. Thank you for joining my listeners and I around the CAMPFIRE (marshmallows not included). Enjoy!

Part I: Ghost Stories

The meat and potatoes of any good campfire tale-telling session are ghost stories. Whether it's a mysterious girl in the attic, Lizzie Borden haunting a bed and breakfast, or a long-dead nurse coming back to serve a patient, our CAMPFIRE is no different. Ghost stories are our main stock in trade.

Who knows what ghosts represent? Not I, but I do believe they are real. Are they the spirits of the dearly—or not so dearly—departed, a residual psychic "tape recording" of long-past emotions, or interdimensional travelers? Your guess is as good as mine. After doing these programs for six years, my best educated guess is that no one really knows what is behind the ghost phenomena. Yet that makes it no less real!

What struck me most about these stories as I heard them was the absolute sincerity, and sometimes fear, decades after the experience, that permeated the voices of these callers as they retold their supernatural stories. Read on and you'll see what I mean. These stories are told in the voice of the callers, which I think makes them all the more chilling. Stoke the fire; it's ghost story time!

Chapter 1

Would You Like a Spot of Tea?

The thing is, this is kind of a secondhand story. My partner, Paula, her family...they describe themselves as "spooky." You sometimes meet people who have paranormal stories, and they've got, like, one paranormal story, and then you get a person to whom this happens on a monthly basis. Her whole family is like that. I'm convinced that whatever experience a person sees is as much about him or her as it is about the experience. Her family is willing to see whatever it is that exists as part of the "other world." And I'm sure that whatever it is must be hereditary as well, because I meet so many people whose whole family has had these experiences—and my partner's family, they're into paranormal experiences.

Paula's mum's experience is the most amazing I think I've ever heard. She often has small medical procedures, so she's not particularly well; she goes into the National Health Service (NHS) every now and again. She lives in a place called

Low Hill next to Liverpool, and she was in this NHS ward after an operation with lots of other people there. They were all asleep, and she was up quite late, just not able to get to sleep. A nurse came around and talked to her for a few minutes and asked her if she was okay, and asked her if she wanted a cup of tea. And at this point she said yes, she wanted a cup of tea. There was something about this nurse that seemed quite odd, but she couldn't put her finger on it at the time. The nurse went away, and she didn't come back for ages; actually, I think it was about an hour before she came back with the cup of tea, and by then Paula's mum realized what was strange: She had a kind of old-fashioned uniform on.

Paula's mum asked her, "What's the deal with the old uniform?" The nurse apparently just smiled at her and walked away. The next morning, Paula's mum checked into the nurses that were on duty that night. There was only one nurse on duty that night, and it hadn't been the one in the old-fashioned uniform.

Paula's mum became more and more convinced that she'd actually seen a ghost. These things happened to her quite a lot—spooky things. She sees psychics quite a lot, and this one particular psychic sees her. (I don't really approve of psychics; in my experience they usually turn out to be charlatans.) She asked this guy about the experience. She described what happened and he did whatever psychics do, and he said that he was getting a name. It was Lily. So the next time Paula's mum went into this hospital for another small operation, she engaged one of the nurses in a conversation about, you know, goings-on in this hospital. She told the nurse that she felt that she'd had an experience in this hospital. And the nurse asked, "Oh, what was that?" Paula's mum described it and which ward it was. The nurse went, "Oh, that would have been Lily." It turns out she was the resident ghost.

I think they had a bit of a discussion—but again, I'm getting this secondhand. People who worked at the hospital apparently had done some research because lots of people had seen this nurse. She'd never frightened anybody; she'd gone around and sort of...just asked people if they needed any help, and if they wanted a cup of tea. Whether she'd made all these people cups of tea, I'm not quite sure. You know, we've all heard of a ghost talking to people, but never preparing food! I said to her, "You should have tried to push it as far as you could go; try to get a latte or something."

I'm 51 now, and, you know, nurses now wear these horrible blue sacks; they're terrible. But when I was a kid the uniforms were quite sexy, with big skirts and little hats. I guess they have to wear these things, but it's a loss!

Dave
United Kingdom

Chapter 2

Wheezer

When I was in college I was a member of a fraternity. Our frat house was this huge mansion at least 100 years old, with the classic legend of a ghost in the house. The story goes back to the 1920s when the owner and his wife lived in the old house: Apparently there was some intermingling between one of the servants and the lord of the mansion, and the female servant had gotten pregnant. And supposedly the owner, to suppress knowledge of it, murdered the servant.

Fast-forward to when I was there: The ghost in the house was known as Wheezer because people reported hearing this wheezing sound at night; it was really kind of a spooky thing. A lot of these stories were circulating around the house, and I personally had friends who told me that they had heard this wheezing sound. People had seen curtains moving when the windows were shut tight and things like that. This was a real scary thing and I was wondering what was going on.

I stayed on the third floor with the president of the fraternity for three or four nights, and he had this batting helmet from the New York Yankees hanging on a nail on the wall. At about 10 o'clock, three out of the four nights that week that we were there, that batting helmet flew off the wall and rolled across the floor. It did not fall straight down, Jim; it flew across the room and rolled. We would look at each other and say, "Oh my gosh, that's Wheezer!"

Jeff
Pennsylvania

Chapter 3

Guess Who Came to Dinner

From when we first moved into our house, my husband and I had the feeling that there was something going on in our home. The very first incident occurred when we were having dinner. We had a bag near our refrigerator where we keep recyclables, and both of us witnessed this bag swinging on its own. There was no breeze. Nothing. But the bag started moving, and it startled us both. Things started occurring after that...things that I would almost describe as curious, as though something was just watching us because we were new in the home.

My husband and I had experiences when we felt like we were being touched. Again, one time at dinner my husband had just started eating, and he said, "Someone just touched me on the back." Another time, I was painting—I'm an artist—and I was doing some work at my art table. I had gotten really close to look at what I was doing and when I moved back to kind of observe it, I felt that I had pushed into somebody, like someone had been looking over my shoulder. I felt this distinct feeling that something was there. And we had other things—noises, the TV turning off; you know, things of that sort that happened.

There was one day, or one evening I should say, I was asleep with my husband, and we had a cat in the bed with us, and all of us were startled awake with what sounded like a clipboard slamming on the ground. I often put my paintings on clipboards, so we got up and checked out my studio area, and there was nothing out of place. But it was a loud enough crash to wake us all up.

Honestly, I never felt there was anything bad about it; there was nothing malevolent. The entity just seemed more curious about us than anything else. It wasn't bad.

The house does have something of a curious history. It was built in the 1950s, and actually started out as some kind of an outdoor shelter. The family that owned the property decided to make it into a cabin, so it was built by the father and his wife and sons, and the sons more or less grew up in the house. Curiously enough, we did some remodeling a few months ago that involved replacing the tile in the bathroom, and we found the initials of the kids who had helped build the house in the concrete. So our thought was, *Maybe the entity was the older gentleman that had helped build the house in the beginning.*

If whoever or whatever it is left, I'd be sad. I really would. The incidents have kind of slowed down a bit, but we're starting to hear noises again. I think he's making a return.

I'm pretty much grounded in science. I would say that before all of this I had been a skeptic, but always open to it... open to the idea that there's energy in the world and that energy can neither be created nor destroyed, so where does that go? I guess I can accept it from a scientific perspective.

My family thinks the idea of a haunting is very credible. In fact, I had my sister and her family up for a summer after it first started happening, and my two little nephews refused to come in the house alone. They believe that something lives here.

Chris

Minnesota

Chapter 4

It Was Just the Cat

When I was growing up, we had quite a large yellow cat. Family pet. When she was getting on in years, she became ill, so we had to put her down. I'm a skeptical person, and I haven't had many ghostly experiences or anything, but about a month after we put her to sleep, my mother and I were talking to each other in the living room, a few feet apart, and the strangest thing happened.

I know what I saw. I'm not sure what *she* saw, but I saw something pet-sized dart in between us, running between our legs, and both of us looked down at the same moment. I asked, "What was that?" And not thinking of the implications of what she was saying, she blurted out, "Oh, it was just the cat."

But the thing of it is, the cat had already passed on, as I mentioned, so it was very odd. I wouldn't have believed it if it had just been me, but she was also there and we both reacted to it. It was interesting, to say the least.

Heidi
New York

Chapter 5

Calling Out the Spirits

I live in Minnesota and recently visited Lilydale Park. It's very near the famed Wabasha Street Caves, which are supposedly extremely dangerous and have signs all over that say so. Lilydale Park is apparently haunted.

The whole adventure started with my buddy Kevin. He had a film class in college and his project was to make a documentary. He decided to do one on ghost hunting. That was absolutely up my alley! I jumped all over it and said, "Absolutely, let's do it."

The night we went there it was dead quiet at first. Nothing. It seemed very calm. There were no loud animal noises. It was in the dead of winter, so I'm sure they were all sleeping by that time. But the first odd thing that happened actually did have to do with an animal.

I've always been a big fan of the *Ghost Adventures* show on Travel Channel so I took a page out of out of Zak Bagans's book: I tried to do a little intimidation. The Lilydale Park area is near St. Paul, but it's in the middle of nowhere St. Paul, so a lot of really bad things like crime happen in the area. There's a lot of bad energy.

So, the first thing I did was to call out any evil spirits that were there. Suddenly, we heard this incredibly strange howling noise. I've never heard a dog howl like that, and I don't know why a wolf or coyote would be in the middle of St. Paul. It kind of set the tone for the night. Then we walked down the trails, asked questions, and did a little EVP (electronic voice phenomenon) work.

There is a center trail that kind of forks to the left and to the right. You could clearly see where it was because the ground was very white. Me and my buddy Kevin were walking down the trail, just not paying attention, looking straight ahead. All of a sudden, the last part of the trail went completely black and then became white again.

We didn't hear any movement—*nothing*. It just went black. Me, being the skeptic, I went down there to investigate. There were no trees, so there's no chance that the trail got blacked out by the trees, because (a) I wasn't moving, and (b) there weren't any branches there. So that was another strange but interesting part of the evening.

Later on, after we were pretty much done, we were ready to get in the car, and I asked one last thing. I just asked if there was any evidence that we may have caught that we didn't realize, and probably a minute and a half later, there was a sound. We were standing by some steel barriers and it sounded like someone took a sledgehammer to it—right next to us.

I listened to the EVP that we recorded thousands of times. The only thing that I can get out of it is, "Will you save me?" It's perfect.

Our little ghost-hunting adventure piqued my interest, if nothing else. I am planning a trip to Waverly Hill Sanatorium in Kentucky. It is supposedly haunted!

Bob

Minnesota

Chapter 6

Minuteman on Guard

I was about 13 years old this time I had a friend over. We lived in an old house. It was built around 1850, and there was a shed behind it that was the original house that was built in the 1700s. My father was using it as a shed and it also functioned as a garage.

Anyway, it was time for my friend to go home, and she needed a ride because it was about 9 o'clock in the evening and dark out. She and I walked out to the car ahead of my father, thinking he'd be out in a few minutes. When we got out there together, it was very dark.

We looked into the shed/garage to go open the car doors. In front of the car, as big as life, we both saw a glowing green Revolutionary War soldier! We saw it at the same time, because we looked at each other and went, "Wha—? Did you see that?" Both of us!

We turned around and ran back into that house like we were on fire—hysterical 13-year-old girls. We ran up to my father and said, "You've got to see this, blah blah blah! We're not going back out there!" He just kind of chuckled at us and said, "Oh, you guys are silly." Of course, when he walked back out there with us, there wasn't anything there.

There were some other tales around town but nothing like what we experienced. There was a house in the same town that was even older, from the early 1700s, owned by one of the town founders. Supposedly, they had had to house some Hessian soldiers in the basement there. They would have been prisoners of war; they were German mercenaries. So there was a little bit of a history in our town of people from that time period who may not have died under the best circumstances. On the property where I grew up there was actually a sort of little family cemetery plot. My grandparents, when they bought the house, removed the headstones.

It was 30 years ago now, but it was kind of burned into my memory. I remember sort of a lime-green light, and darker portions that were enough that you could make out some features, you know, like the shadows of someone having a coat on, and maybe a belt. There was enough detail. It was sort of like if you looked at a sepia-toned photograph or something, except instead of being brown it was green. And it was a vibrant light, because it drew our attention. Looking into a completely dark shed, it was like, *Whoa, there it is.*

It's kind of funny, because people kind of laugh at you and they say, "Oh, that can't happen," but I've also met other people who claim to have seen spirits. I love to ask them, "Was it green and glowing?" A lot of times they'll say yes, which always makes me feel sort of vindicated, you know?

Katie
Connecticut

Chapter 7

The Groaning Ghost

I was living in a small farmhouse in a very, very remote area in northern Minnesota, and my boyfriend at the time and I were asleep. We were woken out of a dead sleep by something that went "UHHH." Right outside the bedroom door. And we just instantly said, "What the heck was that??" We were thinking, *Was it the wind? No, the wind's not blowing. Was it this? Was it that?*

It was so loud that it kind of reverberated, from what I remember. We got ourselves settled down, and kind of calmed down a little bit and talked about it, and went back to sleep. As soon as we got to sleep again, it went "UHHH." Right outside the bedroom door again. It was weird, and it was so loud it vibrated the door of the bedroom.

This was in 1985, and I still think about it constantly. And I wonder, *What could it be?* And I'm a total debunker. I tried to think of every possible thing it could be, and I can't think of anything.

Well, the area was settled in the late 1800s by a Finnish family, and the house that I was in was about 60 years old at the time. I know that because my dad actually spent time with his friend who lived in the house when he was a small boy. But there was another house on the property that burned to the ground before that. Whether anyone died in that house I don't know.

There was that instance, and then there was another when I was home by myself. It was just me and my German shepherd and my cat, and I was lying in bed reading, wide awake, and all of a sudden it sounded like someone was stomping around in my basement wearing wooden clogs. And the first thing I thought was, *Why is there a horse in my basement?* It was crazy, it was that loud. And my shepherd went up to the top of the basement stairs, and her hair was standing up and she was snarling. I was petrified.

That clomping noise probably went on—it probably seemed like it went on longer than it did—but I would guess it went on for about 10 seconds. I tried to re-create that sound in the basement—and again, it was super loud, just like that voice that yelled at me—so, I don't know. It scared my dog; it scared me half to death. I think if it were to happen now, I think I wouldn't be so scared, probably partly from listening to your show.

Keeley
Minnesota

Chapter 8

Goodnight, Grandpa

When I was a kid, my grandmother watched us a lot. The night of my grandfather's funeral, I decided to spend the night at my grandmother's house the way I usually did. When my grandfather was alive, there was almost a ritual that he would perform: In the middle of the night, he'd walk down the hall and go into the kitchen. I'd be sleeping on the couch. From my vantage point there, I could see into the kitchen. He'd go in for a piece of fruit or something like that and then he would walk back up the hall. I'd awaken slightly and usually hear him crunch into an apple or something as he was walking back up the hall going back to bed.

As I mentioned, the night of his funeral, I decided to spend the night there, because I just wanted to feel closer to him. For some reason, in the middle of the night I woke up because I heard somebody walking down the hall, and

I wasn't sure if my grandmother was getting up for something. I know I was awake because I pretty much sat up on the couch and waited for her to come down the hall, but she never did.

All of a sudden there was a light on in the kitchen, as if someone had opened the fridge. And was thinking, *Okay...* I was sitting there waiting, and the light went off, and I didn't see anyone come out of the kitchen. It was light enough in the house that you could see someone walking in and out of the kitchen. After the light shut off I heard someone walking down the hall, and I heard a crunch, like an apple being bitten into. So I just kind of rolled over, said "Goodnight, Grandpa," and went back to sleep.

I have absolutely no doubt in my mind that there is so much more after this life. In the years since, I've had a chance to process it, and the experience has really helped me deal with any kind of loss in my life, because I know that they're still here, you know what I mean? I'm sad that they're gone, but I can say goodbye to them and feel as though I'm going to see them again.

Thomas
Illinois

Chapter 9

The Girl in the Attic

When I was about 9 or 10 years old, my best friend in the world was one of the neighborhood boys, named Hubert. His family had invited me to go with them on a long weekend to visit some of their relatives, so I went. I'm not really sure where we went, but it couldn't have been very far; it was just a couple hours' drive. Not much about the weekend was that memorable, to tell you the truth. I don't remember much about the family either. Of course, being a young boy, I wasn't aware of much anyway.

So anyway, we got there, Hubert and I. He was usually the one who was more inquisitive; he'd do things...he was mischievous, in other words. So, at one point, we decided to go up to the attic and play. The one thing I remember about the attic is that it was very clean and sparse. There wasn't a whole lot to do up there.

We got up there, and noticed that there was a little girl in the attic. This little girl, she wanted to stay in one corner of the attic, like that was her space, and she didn't want to come down and really play with us much. I remember at one point we had maybe a ball or something that we were tossing around, and we'd toss it to her. She'd never respond.

She never talked. She had long hair, and I never saw her face; it was strange. Never saw her face. She had long hair that basically just covered her face. It came down probably to the middle of her chest. And I remember she was wearing maybe a white sundress or a gown of some sort. Her clothes seemed modern. That's my feeling about it.

So, after trying to play some ball with her, we decided...I think there was a table, so we were going to play some cards or checkers, something like that. We got her to join us at the table, and she was just sitting there with us. We'd make our moves, and she was just sitting there, not doing anything. She didn't talk, and I don't remember seeing her face. It was kind of like the girl in *The Ring*. At the time, I was a kid and I thought, *She's no fun; she doesn't want to play with us*.

Well, in addition to how strange she was acting, my memory of her is not of fluid movement; it's not like she actually moved. She didn't seem ghostly, like ethereal or something like that; I just remember that she was in the corner and she wouldn't play with us, and then all of a sudden she was at the table. Kind of herky-jerky; it was almost like snapshots of her.

Well, the family...that's what led me to believe that something strange was going on, because I remember after we did what we were going to do in the attic, we got bored with it or whatever, and came downstairs. I remember watching a movie with the family and even having dinner with them later that night, and the girl wasn't there. She wasn't there with the family at any point! If the girl was for real, she would have been there with the family. At that point it dawned on me: *Oh God, we've been playing with a ghost!* That's the only conclusion I could come up with, really.

If he listens to the podcast: Why don't you call up, Hubert? Maybe he could fill in some of the holes for us. I haven't been in touch with him since. They moved away.

Lindsay
North Carolina

Chapter 10

Civil War Phantoms

I grew up in Mechanicsville, Virginia, with my family—my two siblings and parents. Our property was located on the actual battlefield where the battle of Beaver Dam Creek took place. It was a major engagement during the American Civil War. If you were to go outside and sit on my front porch, you would be less than a quarter of a mile to the actual marker of this battlefield that claimed well more than 1,000 casualties.

Oddly enough, I never associated my experiences within the house with the battle until I got older and became interested in the paranormal. And it just seemed kind of strange that very peculiar things happened to me as a kid growing up in this house, because the battlefield was so close to where we lived.

The first thing that happened to me in this house, the first thing that I noticed, was in the early to mid-1990s. I was somewhere between 8 and 12 years old. As I would go to sleep every night, I would hear breathing. This was human breathing: inhales, exhales...it was clear as day, and it would happen multiple times throughout the week. There's nothing else I could have mistaken it for—there was no central air in the house, no fans, nothing. It sounded exactly like breathing. Almost every other night I would just listen to it, and it would scare the hell out of me.

I told my parents about it, and they didn't really believe me. Quite a few things actually happened in that house, but they didn't experience anything. It seemed to only gravitate toward me and my room, which was really strange. Perhaps it's because kids are more susceptible to these types of things.

One interesting incident happened when I was about 11 years old. It was a typical summer and we were out all day climbing trees and having fun. I'd jumped from one branch to another and lost my grip; as I fell back I tried to break my fall with my arm, and I broke it. I ran home crying. My parents didn't quite believe that I had actually broken it, so they wanted to wait until the next day before they went and got the X-ray.

That night, they put me in my sister's room for the evening because it's closer to their bedroom and the bed was easier to get into with my hurt arm. So I was lying there in the middle of the night (I didn't know it at the time, but I did have a broken arm). I was there with my arm elevated, and the house was totally still. Not a sound. All of a sudden, I heard footsteps start from the beginning of the hallway, and they were coming in the direction of the bedroom.

I was lying in the bed, parallel to the wall that meets the hallway and near the open door to the hallway. I listened to the noise come closer and closer—and it was unmistakable; they were definitely footsteps—and as the footsteps landed directly in front of my room, right where my head was, near the door, I screamed loudly for my mother. She jumped out of bed and asked, "What's going on?" She reassured me that no one was up; it couldn't have been anybody—but I heard it. Someone or something was walking straight down the hallway, as clear as day.

Well, growing up we, would always hear the schoolyard stories about hearing cannon fire, or gun shots, those types of things. I never experienced anything like that. I did, as I got into the paranormal, try to look into it myself, and I wasn't able to find anything. I even asked—you know, as an adult—I asked my siblings, "Did you experience anything in this house?" And no, nothing at all. But I know something sure happened to me.

Daniel
Virginia

Chapter 11

The Home of Gathered Spirits

In my opinion, all of Hawaii is pretty spooky. A lot of people think of Hawaii as just a paradise, but I've always been surprised that the paranormal community hasn't caught on to the fact that an incredible amount of activity happens here, and has historically for a long time. The place where I live on the island of Oahu is a valley called Nuuanu Valley, and it's just full of stuff always going on.

Of all the stories I have, the one I think is most interesting is what happened to my girlfriend, because she's not particularly into the paranormal. She's not a believer—she's not an unbeliever; she's a physicist, you know? Her world is very cut and dried. She's a scientist. But she's also really sensitive to these things. She picks up on stuff, and she'll tell me about things, and I'll be very surprised, and she'll just think these are anomalous things that happen.

I'll say, "Wow, that's amazing, how could you not be super-excited about this, or be thinking about it?" But, as I said, she's such a scientist and it doesn't even register that way to her.

One of my favorite stories is when we lived in this old house deep in the valley, which was in the jungle. A lot of interesting people have lived there. We had this lower part of the house, in the jungle, where you could see through our bedroom into a hallway, into another bedroom past that. One night, I was asleep and she looked down that hallway and she saw a man. A shadow of a man. It wasn't clear; it was an apparition; this dark thing that she could tell was a man by the shadow. It was unnaturally tall, probably 6 or 7 feet tall, and very lean looking. She just automatically had the feeling that it was a man, a male presence, that was sort of passing through the room.

What she thought was even more strange—and I agreed—was that at the exact moment she was seeing that happen, she heard a voice. It was a female voice, not talking to her, but talking to the apparition. The woman's voice said, "What are you doing here?"

When my girlfriend told me the story, I asked, "What do you mean?" She's was just candid about it: "I saw this man and he was passing through, and the moment I looked and saw this thing, I heard a woman's voice in my ear speaking to it, saying, 'What are you doing here?'"

Now, one thing that she tells me, the thing I should tell you about this that makes it even more interesting, has to do with her. She rides the bus to and from work, and on the bus you find interesting characters, obviously. She mentioned to me once that she was talking to a woman who was a little bit crazy, but quite lucid—one of those people you think could have one foot in one world and one in the other. This woman said that this particular place where we were living in the valley is a type of cache for lost spirits, and what happens is that lost spirits get caught up in the valley and get blown out—like a spiritual energy will come and then blow out the same way that leaves will get stuck at the eddy of a stream or something, and then the current will increase and push them out.

This strange woman said that, at times, when a lot of spirits get caught in that area, then activity goes up. I just thought, *Well, doesn't that sort of sound like what happened? This female presence, and maybe this tall male presence, maybe they're just sort of wandering around wondering what the other is doing there.*

This house that we lived in was almost in a complex, in a very old part of the neighborhood—a very nice part, so it was one where you wouldn't normally have strange tenants. But this 80-year-old man who ran the place was a really nice guy who would take in different people. We had about 12 people living in this place—all different kinds. There were three different houses, and three of the women who lived there were practicing witches. They were just casual about it, and they would come in and say, "Oh, we feel a weird energy around the property, so we're just going to smudge and do that sort of thing." I'm not necessarily into that, but it doesn't bother me and I'm open to whatever. But they were matriarchal, these three witches; they took care of the property and of this old man who had allowed them to stay there.

When he finally passed, he was seen after his death—by everybody. I saw him. They saw him. He was just sort of taking one last stroll through his house. The interesting thing was that it wasn't surprising. It was just expected. And this was after his body had been removed. The ambulance had come to take him away. Later that day, he was seen just sort of standing in various places in the house.

Travis
Hawaii

Chapter 12

The Late, Great Captain George

I am in the sound business, and about six years ago I was installing a PA system in a theater in Georgetown, Prince Edward Island. It's a small community about two hours away from where I live, and the building was called King's

Play House. This building has quite a history to it. It was kind of like a town hall that had burned down a couple of times. Recently the local ghost-hunter society has begun an investigation because of new information that has shown up about this building, that it was actually built on a graveyard several years ago. So, there's lots more history coming out as it goes along.

Getting back to my story, I was doing an installation for a sound company, and the first day I showed up at the job site, the person who was letting me in didn't tell me too much history about the building; I just commented on how it had character and stuff like that, and then he wouldn't enter the building as I was getting ready to do the job. He left me with instructions on where to go and what to do. So I worked for a couple of hours and I didn't notice anything odd. Then, I noticed as I was going through a room that it was just very very cold in this room, and the chimney had been cold in the furnace room. And then I went to one area of the room and it was probably a 30-degree temperature drop from one step to the next. It was very, very drastic. I just kind of blew it off; didn't think anything about it. Again, it's an old building with character.

It seemed that I was always seeing something out of the corner of my eye, whether it was a shadow or just something that wasn't right. The biggest thing that really set me off in this whole installation was when I was doing some work and I put my electric drill onto the charger. I turned around and that drill and charger were gone, and I'm thinking, *Didn't I just put this here?* Of course, it was during a long day, so I chalked it up to the possibility that I put it in another area of the building. But lo and behold, I turned around about five minutes later and it was back, right in the center of the room where I had originally put it. So that was one of those...issues...that just kind of...where I said, *You know, either I'm getting real tired from doing this job, or there's something up here.*

I guess the final thing that set me off was going into rooms and lights coming on and going off. And again, that's not the first time I've had that happen in buildings that are old—the electrical can be a little bit strange. But there was just a little too much interesting to this, so...

After I finished the job, I learned a bit more about this place. I'd had my wrap-up with the person who had hired me to do it, and he said, "So, did you notice anything different?" I said, "Well, yeah, there were a couple of strange things." I didn't say anything about specific incidents. He said, "Well, the building's haunted." I said, "Yeah, that really does make sense," and I explained everything that had happened. I'd also explained how the gentleman who was letting me into the building wouldn't enter the building. It turned out that this guy was purely petrified of the paranormal and had just had some experiences himself in there, and just didn't want to go in. But as Town Alderman he had keys to the building, and he does carry on some of the business for it. So, he had to be there, but he wouldn't cross the threshold of the building. That kind of summed it up nicely to me.

One other thing: They had actually put a name to the ghost. They call it Captain George, who was a sea captain in the area, where the community used to be famous for ship-building there on the island, years and years ago. Apparently, he was either captain of a ship that went down, or something happened...anyway, they presume that's who's haunting the building right now. They actually also have a reserved seat in the theater for him. They will not sell this seat; it's specifically for this gentleman, and people have noticed since they've done that that the appearances have been less and less, but whenever they sell that seat, strange things happen.

Anything's possible. There's so much in this world that we can't explain, and like I said, there were too many coincidences on that job site for me to chalk it up to being tired, or this or that. There was something going on there, you could feel it. It was just a different feeling.

Chris
Canada

Chapter 13

Bullmoose Is Back!

I have had many varied paranormal experiences, but I thought this was a good one because it affects people other than myself.

I was working at a small indie record company in Pittsburgh called Bogus Records back in the 1980s, and I'm a graphic designer, so I was doing little things like promotional materials and posters on a volunteer basis. Carl, who's the owner of the company, was having a summer party for his employees and talent. He is quite an individual, and he is a crazy collector. And he was kind enough to give a friend and me a tour of his house because we'd never been there before. He had a room full of arcade games, like the old Pac-Man...remember the 1980s games?

Anyway, he took us through his fantastic Beatles memorabilia, and he even had a rubber alligator in his bathtub. I tell you, this guy was crazy. And he took us to his office, and there was a whole wall full of head shots of all the people he'd worked with and managed, and so on and so forth. After the tour, we went back down and did the party thing.

That night, I had this dream that I was in a local record store that was near my house. But unlike the real record store, the front area had kind of a lounge area with two couches and a coffee table. I'm standing in the store looking through—in those days—vinyl albums (if we all remember those). This little man comes up to me and he starts kind of yelling at me, very agitated, like, "Where is it??" and "Why isn't it done?" I look at him and say, "I don't know what you're talking about." He kind of huffs to the front of the store and I follow him, and he's kind of standing behind one of those couches and still kind of, you know, reaming my butt out for this...whatever it was.

In the dream, I just listen very politely and in a few minutes Carl and Phil, who also worked at the studio, they walk into the store. They're kind of standing behind the other couch nearest the door, and we exchange greetings, and the man—the little man that I'd been talking to—asks me something, so I respond to what his query was. Carl and Phil turn to me and ask, "Who are you talking to?" I just look at them as if they're crazy and say, "I'm talking to Bullmoose! Don't you see him?" They kind of look at me and laugh like I'm nuts, and inform me, "Well, you know, Bullmoose is dead."

Just then I was realizing that, *Oh, this is a special dream.* I have lucid dreams a lot, and I knew how to amp myself up, and I told myself that I had to really start remembering details on this.

Phil and Carl ask me what he was saying, in a smart-butt kind of way, and I pretty much say that "Bullmoose is very agitated and he wants you to finish it." And they respond with, "Finish what?" I really wasn't sure either, but Bullmoose keeps saying, "The record! The record! The record!" They look at each other, figuring I'm trying to pull a fast one on them. They ask me, "Okay, which songs weren't finished on that album?" Bullmoose, of course, relays me the information, and in my dream I'm thinking, in my lucid way, *I have to remember the names of these songs. I have to.* I relay the songs to Carl and Phil, and they look at each other, shocked. They turn white, looking almost confused and freaked out. Then they walk out of the record store.

And that, pretty much, was the end of that part of the dream. The dream changes to Bullmoose sitting on the corner on a stool, singing me a sweet little lullaby, thanking me for relaying the information.

Of course, the next morning I woke up and I wrote down everything I could, especially the titles of the songs, because I have a brain like a sieve, and I could only remember one full title and most of the second one. The third one I couldn't remember at all. But it was a really long dream, as you can tell.

Although I knew this was an important dream, I didn't feel compelled to go calling people up about it. I just try to let the universe take its course, and when the right time presents itself, I know to do something about it.

A week, maybe two weeks later, I was down at the recording studio, and I was working with Phil on some poster designs. He was in a hurry, and he didn't have a lot of time; he had a meeting he had to make, and in the back of my head, I'm going, *Damn it, I knew there was something I wanted to tell him!* I just...I couldn't remember at all.

I followed him up the stairs, and as soon as the sunlight hit me, for some reason it all came back to me. And I turned to him, as Phil started to head down the street, and I just said, "Phil, is there...on Carl's wall of head shots..." and I drew a diagram in the air, "right about in the middle. Is there a head shot of a little black guy with big glasses, kind of a long face, and is his name Bull-something?" I couldn't remember his name. "And, um, is he dead?" Phil just looked at me and stopped and said, "Yeah, why do you ask?" I said, "Because he wants you to know that he wants that record done."

At that, Phil was like, "What are you talking about?" So, I related my dream, and he was kind of taken aback. Then he asked me if I remembered the titles of the songs that needed to be finished. I said, "I can tell you two of them," and I told him what I remembered the titles being, and I swear that Phil turned white as a sheet right there on the street. I mean, he was...at first you could see that he was shaken, but then he got a little indignant, like "Who told you that?" As if someone had slipped me some, you know... information.

I said, "Bullmoose told me; I just told you that!" Phil was still kind of skeptical, and he said, "Well, you must have heard it from somebody." I had actually been considering that all along, but there was no connection with any of these people involved. So Phil ended up going off to his appointment very visibly shaken, and I went home. As Phil related it to me later, I guess that night he went over to Carl's house and they were in his kitchen and he told Carl all about my dream and as much of the details as he could remember, and, of course, Carl naturally laughed, scoffed, and pretty much figured that I was BS-ing Phil. I guess Carl was laughing at my tall tale when, just then, dishes fell off the cupboard and crashed to the floor.

And as Phil said to me, he looked at Carl and then looked at the dishes, and Carl looked at him and looked at the dishes. They looked at each other, they looked at the dishes, and Carl went to the phone and said he figured he'd better do something about this, so he started making arrangements to get this album started.

Ever since I had that dream, I had felt this connection to Bullmoose. Almost as if he were with me, kind of in me. Not that he was overshadowing me or...and I'm careful, cautious about those kinds of things, but it was like I could...every once in a while, I would just look in a mirror and say, "Hey Bullmoose, what's it like to be a little green-eyed Scotch-German girl? It must be a real trip for you!" And it was just... one of those kinds of things that I just kept feeling he was there, but I never had any proof of it. There's nothing he ever overtly did that made me really feel that he was with me; it was just a feeling.

Well, months later, I went to a CD release party for a local band called The Spuds, a great Pittsburgh band. I hadn't talked to anybody about the status of Bullmoose's album, whether it was finished, or what had been done. I just let the universe do its thing, and I was outside listening to the band at this party. Suddenly I just started crying and I started feeling a spirit lifting out of my body, like right out of my solar plexus, just this...it's so hard to describe, but it was like a part of me, but like a separation. And the feeling of this entity or this spirit or whatever—this thing was just full of joyousness, happiness, and gratitude. It totally made me giddy, yet I was crying. It was a crazy, powerful feeling. It was just so wonderful, and I really knew it was Bullmoose, like, *Dang it, he was inside of me all this time!*

It seemed as though Bullmoose was thanking me for helping him—right in the middle of this release party. I wasn't yet sure why though. He communicated that he was going to rest, and at last he felt he was free to go. After composing myself, I walked over to Phil, who was standing near me, and I was still really quite overwhelmed, and I asked him, "Did you finish the album?" and he turned to me and said that they'd just put the album to bed. All I could say was, "Bullmoose says 'thank you.'"

Sandy
California

Chapter 14

Our Family Dog

Our family dog had gotten quite old, so we had to put her down. After that is when things started happening.

After she was gone, it was like she really wasn't. During the night you'd hear her moving around—her claws on the floor, scratching on the front door, stuff like that. My other family members would hear things as well; my sister heard it and so did my parents. I didn't feel frightened.

One day as I was rounding the corner into the kitchen, I almost felt that I'd bumped into her lying around. It was just like before, when she was still alive and you walked past her. You could feel her walking by too, after she passed away.

As I said, I wasn't frightened or anything; it was a comforting feeling at the time.

She hasn't been around as much recently, actually. It's been very quiet around here; nothing from her. But there's a feeling that she's still around, keeping an eye on us or protecting us or something. It's like she's just hanging around.

Chris
Sweden

Chapter 15

My Roommate, Lizzie Borden

About a year ago, I had a boyfriend who was very into everything paranormal, just as I have always been. So for his birthday, I decided to take him to Lizzie Borden's Bed and Breakfast, which is located in Fall River, Massachusetts. We were really pumped up about going on this trip; very excited. We didn't know much about Lizzie Borden, but we thought it was going to be fun. So we got there, and as soon as we walked in, there was just kind of this really strange feeling, just a very heavy feeling overall.

The first thing they do there is take you on a tour of the house. They tell you the story about how Lizzie Borden supposedly killed her mother and father, and they tell you things that have happened to them in the hotel as well—and then they send you off to bed, of course.

A few things have happened to me with ghosts and spirits in the past, so I was a little bit nervous, and of course I bought all these gifts for my boyfriend that were, like, board games and things, so we wouldn't have to sleep that night. Right away, he started complaining about how tired he was. So I said, "Okay, we can go to bed, but here are the rules: You have to sleep with your back to me, we cannot turn off the lights, and I don't want you to go to sleep until you hear me snoring." So, we lay down to go to sleep, and of course, immediately I hear him snoring. So I was like, *Great, I'm here all by myself now.*

So I'm lying there, getting ready to sleep, when all of a sudden I feel something pick up my toes, lift my foot up, and then drop it. And I thought, *Hmmm...that's kind of strange. All right, I know that I'm still awake, I know that the lights are on, I know that I'm under the covers, nothing could have grabbed my leg without me noticing. I'm just going to ignore it and try to go back to sleep.* So I lie back down, and again a few minutes later, I feel something pick up my toes, lift up my foot, and drop it.

And I thought, *Something is definitely, definitely going on here.*

As soon as you walk into the place, there's just this feeling that something really, really bad had happened. We were so excited beforehand, but as soon as we walked in the door, we could tell something was going on.

We felt a spirit in the bathroom as well. We took our turns taking a shower, and we both came to the conclusion without saying anything to the other one that there was definitely kind of a...it felt as though somebody was staring at you the whole time. The feeling from the bathroom was a really heavy, kind of evil feeling, but the one in the bedroom picking up the foot, that was totally a playful, fun spirit.

One of the women there, the one who owns it, said that something had happened to her in that room as well; one day she had been fixing up the room for the next set of guests, and something went through her body and knocked her on the ground. That was actually the room where the murder of the mother had happened.

It was spooky, but since that experience, I've definitely been on the search for my next haunted bed and breakfast.

Gwynne
New York

Chapter 16

A Night Visitor

After some spooky experiences that my wife, Christina, had, my daughter started asking questions about ghosts and those kind of things. Just for fun, I decided at Halloween time to book us a trip on one of these little ghost tours they do downtown. A lot of cities do this.

There's a little town near us called Bisbee, in Arizona. It is a little mining town, and they have these ghost tours, as well as the Copper Queen hotel, which is pretty famous for being haunted. My stepdad, who has passed away, had stayed there years before, and had told us when we were younger that it was haunted. So I thought that would be a really fun tour to do around Halloween. Well, Halloween is crazy booked, so we couldn't get in, but we got in in November. We walked this huge loop around town, heard a bunch of ghost stories, and took lots of pictures—you know, it was real fun.

We had a nice day and got back to the room and settled down for the night. The day had been pretty uneventful, but we had a fun time. Christina woke me up about maybe 3:30 or 4 in the morning, and said, "Listen, do you hear that?" I woke up and mumbled, "Uh huh, yeah, I hear something." I really wanted to go back to sleep because it was 4 in the morning. And she said, "No, wait; listen. You have to listen to it." It sounded just like a rocking chair on a wooden floor, right by the bed. And this hotel, it's...I guess it's four floors. We stayed on the third floor, and all of our floors were carpeted. It's been renovated, but the hotel is from the 1890s, I guess. Anyway, it sounded just like a rocking chair on a wooden floor. We tried to figure out what it was after that, and we just couldn't.

Shortly after that, Christina had gotten up to go to the restroom, and I heard another sound. I was still actively listening. I heard a woman's voice, a whisper, go through one ear and out the other ear. I mean, Christina wasn't anywhere near me, and there was a woman's voice going around my head. When Christina came back to the bed, I could smell the scent of a perfume, like a rosewater perfume. Like an Old South perfume. Christina lay down in the bed and she asked, "Do you smell that?" Plus, she said she heard the same thing—a woman whispering in her ear! We didn't speak to each other for a minute, and we tried to settle ourselves down, and she lay down into bed and kind of did the little comfortable sigh, kind of a "mmm," and then immediately we both heard a man's voice right after that say "mmm"!

She looked at me, and I said, "That wasn't me." She sat up and looked at the end of our bed and said, "There's a man there, and he's taller than you." I got up, and she told me, "Go get the camera." It was on the other side of the room. I got out of bed and walked to the other side of the room. I stopped halfway to the camera, dead in my tracks. I felt this electrical feeling, like a shock going through my body, and I turned back to her and said, "Look at this." All of the hair all over my body was sticking straight up. And I was so excited. We weren't threatened at all, it was just... real. There was somebody else there. I couldn't see him. She kind of saw him. But we both experienced it, and it was really real.

By the time I got the camera, of course, there was nothing there. Later on, the next day, we tried to re-create everything—hear the voices, the smells, everything like that. We went to the next room, the next level, to see if those had wooden floors, and, of course, they didn't. They were plush carpeting, but both of us know what we heard.

The hotel keeps a ghost journal. We went down the next morning and read some things that had been experienced on the same floor, and even in the same room. Past guests had written the very same experience in the exact same room.

Gordon
Arizona

Chapter 17

Mom's Here Again

We think that my mother-in-law haunts the house, or at least comes back and visits periodically.

We see a lot of shadows and things while watching television. Nothing really direct; it's kind of out of the corner of your eye that things fall off the shelf, cabin doors will open, people will get touched...

Actually, it's happened to me a couple of times. Once, I was standing in the kitchen with my husband, and he was cooking something, and I screamed and jumped about four feet forward, and he gave me this look like I was absolutely crazy. And I said, "Someone just tucked in the tag on my shirt!" You know how the tag in your shirt comes out? He's like, "That's something my mom would do!"

We've never had anything threatening happen in the house, so it's all good.

The weirdest thing that's happened was this story: I was coming in the house and had my hands full of bags. To explain this properly I have to describe the layout of the house. There's kind of one of those bay alcove windows for the house and I'm coming up the driveway and I've got my hands full. I look up and it seems as though there's somebody standing in the window looking out. I do the nod-your-head, hey-I'm-coming-in thing, and I get to the door and I put my hand out to open the door and the doorknob turns. The door opens like somebody's opening it, and this is a hard door to open. I have trouble with it. Now, I'm not exactly the biggest person in the world, but you've got to really push the door to open it, and it opens like there's somebody behind it, pulling it open. And I look behind the door, about to say, "Thanks for opening the door!" And, guess what? There's nobody behind the door.

My husband was in the back, in the bedroom, playing a computer game. But no one was behind the door. I shuffled down the hallway real fast with kind of a freaked-out walk, and I said, "The door just opened by itself."

My husband seems okay with it. He'll acknowledge that he sees and hears things, but as far as exactly what he's heard I'm not entirely sure. The other people in the house...a couple people really seem to notice it, but in general it's just me, my husband, and my father-in-law who notice things. I think we pay attention to that, because we're weird. We're the type of people to stay up all night on Halloween and watch the ghost-hunter specials every year.

Dora

Virginia

Chapter 18

The Elevator Man

This happened in about 2000 or 2001, where I work. Me and my coworker had gone to the break room, and when you leave the break room, you have to go down a long hallway to get to the elevator. As we were walking to the elevator, the doors opened and we saw a man in a gray suit with sandy blond hair walking onto the elevator. One thing that puzzled me is that when you go through elevator doors, typically the sensors cause the doors to open up when someone is going through. In this case, they just kept closing. We walked up just a couple seconds later and hit the button, thinking we'd have to wait for another elevator. Well, lo and behold, the same elevator opened up quickly. We both walked into the elevator, which was empty, and the door closed. We both looked at each other quizzically. My coworker asked, "Didn't a man just walk in here?" and I said, "I was thinking the same thing." Needless to say, as soon as we got to our floor and the doors opened, we got out quickly.

I don't know of a lot of activity in the building, but in our suite we've had other coworkers say that when no one was in the office, you could hear somebody typing. Or that they saw something on their screen that looked like someone walking behind them—little things of that nature.

Velma
Texas

Chapter 19

Grandma's Got More Company

My grandmother's house has been in our family for many years, dating back to the 1920s. First my mother's family owned it and then they ended up selling it to the family that would be her cousin's family eventually. So it all kind of stayed in the family. My grandmother—my dad's mother—would always experience different paranormal activity in the house. She would be downstairs in the living room and hear someone walking across the large room above her and it would sound like a man who had a cane. She talked to my mother's family and they said, "Oh yes, that was Uncle Harry; he died in that room and he did have a cane." They speculated that perhaps that was Uncle Harry who had come back to walk around, and look out the window, and so forth.

My grandmother would often see her brother sitting in the kitchen chair, and the only thing was that her brother had died about 20 years prior. She would turn and feel someone in the room with her and there he'd be. She also experienced this in her car when she was driving.

My grandmother was not even an eccentric woman, let alone crazy. She was a very level-headed kind of person, and she just seemed to think that for some reason or another she was very open to those who had gone before coming back and visiting her.

Her daughter, my aunt, also saw a figure standing in the kitchen. We were all there for an evening, I remember, when I was 7 or 8 years old, for a family dinner. My aunt said, "Look over there in the corner! There's a woman standing there with a veil!" No one could see it but my aunt, and she's not a very eccentric person, either. Then we spoke to my mother's family later about that and I guess the woman my aunt described was Uncle Harry's wife who had passed away in that house as well.

My grandmother was never frightened. In fact, she was very disappointed after talking to a person who was a very devout Catholic—and, you know, we're a family of faith too, but this person seemed to say, "You know, you really want to stop this. Why don't you sprinkle some holy water in your house?" And my grandmother did and she said she never had another experience after that. So she was very disappointed. The holy water was kind of a spur-of-the-moment thing with peer pressure and what have you, but she said the phenomena never really scared her and she liked seeing people.

I could never understand why, if these were genuinely kind spirits and indeed the relatives of the people whom she loved, why they were affected by holy water. That didn't really make any sense to me; if they were really just angels or what have you who had gone and just wanted to come back and say hi, why would they be afraid of holy water? Why would that have stopped it?

My grandmother has passed on and we haven't seen her. One time right after my other grandmother died, we messed around with a Ouija board. My brother was about 12 and I was about 14, and we played with it in her room. It really moved, and we just freaked out so badly. I'm definitely a person who is fast, but I've never run so fast in my life. We ran out to the backyard and my brother climbed up on the fence between our backyard and the school. We never messed with that stuff again because it's just not right.

Ingrid
Pennsylvania

Chapter 20

One Messed-Up House

I moved into this house when I was about 7. It was roughly 1983–84. We lived there for about seven years, and we had all kinds of odd happenings. It was a grand house, built in the 1940–1950 time range. At the time, it was a very upscale neighborhood—not so much now, but it was then.

The first thing that happened had to do with the doorbell. There were different chimes for the different doors; the front door had a very elaborate chime. There were different times, especially in the evening, when the chimes would just ring and ring and ring and we'd have to go outside and literally disconnect the wires in order to stop them. You could just look at the door itself or the button and see that it had been physically jammed in and you'd have to dislodge it.

The way that the neighborhood was set up, we did have neighbors, but there was a good distance in between each of you. So, it wasn't as though someone could push it and then step behind a bush or something; it was obviously happening on its own.

In addition to the doorbell, probably the next thing that I can really remember is a phenomenon on the stairs. It was an older home and the stairs were by the front door right in the foyer, and they take you upstairs to the children's bedrooms. The stairs were older, so of course, when you stepped on them, they would creak. What would happen was, say you were on the stairs and you walked up five or six of them. Then at the bottom of the stairs you could feel the vibration of the stairs themselves and you could hear a sound as if someone had just started walking up them behind you. You would get the feeling as if you could turn around and there would be somebody there.

I was young while in this house and I became very angry when this would happen. I would turn around and swat the air behind me as if to shoo it away. Sometimes it would kind of ease up and sometimes it wouldn't, but it made me feel better!

And then there was the couch. We sold that couch last year actually, but we'd had it all these years. The couch was in the formal living room, which was right off the foyer to the left when you came in. That was the room we used for Christmas and that was pretty much it; that was where the expensive furniture and the antiques were. If my mom caught you in that room you were in big trouble! Nobody went in that room. I think I probably sat on that couch maybe 14 times in my life.

We had a portrait of my great-great-great grandfather who was a captain in the Civil War, and it was centered above the couch. Every night there would be a shadow on the couch. It sat in the center of this couch and it had a human shape. It sat there every single night for seven years. And it literally wore a place into the couch. There was a perfect half-moon shape indented in this couch, as if someone had been sitting there night after night watching television. My mother would get on topics of spooky things with people and would show them the couch. It was bizarre!

Another thing that happened in the house concerned the bed in my room. I'm a very, very, very light sleeper, which really pays off when you have a toddler! You don't sleep through anything! I think I was probably 9 or 10 at the time, and I had twin beds in my room at the very top of the stairs. The stairs go up from the foyer and they turn to the left at the landing and go up, and my room was at the very top of that. One night, I was sleeping with my nightlight on and my door open as always, and I felt my bed raise up, as if someone was sitting on my bed, like when your mother comes in to check on you. She checks on you and she may rub your forehead, and then when she stands up the bed lifts. So I rolled over and said, "Momma?" And there was nobody there.

I was not a girlie-girl. I was very much a tomboy, but my mother had very girlie-girl comforters, which were very fluffy and lacey and flowery. On this comforter there was an imprint, a depression, where someone had sat. I was very certain that she had been in there. So I sat up, and I watched the stairs to see if maybe she had gone around the corner to my restroom or to my brother's room, and I sat there for probably 15 minutes just watching, and, of course, she never did show up. I realized that she was never there. But someone had come into my room.

I believe a single family owned the home before us; I think it was a one-owner home, but I can't swear to that. I heard that the family before us had a mother who was an alcoholic, and she was a very angry alcoholic when she drank. So I thought maybe that was, as I look at it now, a motherly thing to do, to sit down on the bed and check on me.

I think the most startling thing that happened that got everybody's attention was that we had a couple of maids at one time who would come in during the day while my parents were working and we were at school. We would come home and they'd watch after us for a couple of hours until my parents came home. It was two sisters. (At one point it had been just one of the sisters, but she was uncomfortable working there by herself for whatever reason, so her sister came and worked with her.)

One day, we came home from school and we found them standing in the front yard looking at the house. That was odd. They explained that they had been in the kitchen and they were washing the dishes or something and talking, when they heard the front door open. As I said, the stairs going up to our bedrooms are at the front door, and they heard footsteps go up the stairs, and then they heard running across the hallways upstairs. They heard all three of the doors slam (there's three kids' rooms). The sisters had then gone to the foot of the stairs and said, "Children, come down, give us some sugar; how was your day?"

Of course, we never came down, and they realized that it was about 1 o'clock in the afternoon, which was a couple of hours too early for us to be out of school. They went outside and they did not go back in the house and they would not work in the house anymore from that point on, unless the family was there. The only time they ever came to do any work was if my parents had a party or something and they would come over to help out.

One more thing about that house: I found out that the original contractor of that house—I don't know his name, and this could be hearsay; it's a small town—but the original contractor of that house, they say he hanged himself in the house while it was being built. I don't know whether that's true; I can't swear to it, but there you go.

The house changes hands about every five to seven years or so. I can't tell you for sure why it changes hands so many times, but I know for us, I think it was just time. When my husband and I married the house was for sale and we've been married now for a little over five years and it's up for sale again. It's just like clockwork, and at a price that's ridiculously low. It just makes you think.

Beth
North Carolina

Chapter 21

The Haunted Beauty Shop

I was on management at a beauty shop. I would open and close the store, and it would just be me and a receptionist—sometimes just me. We had a practice of locking the door when we counted money out and stuff like that. Anyhow, we would always hear the front door open by itself. When it was locked. After hours.

At first I thought, *Oh, it's my imagination*, and then we would hear the back door—with a push bar on it; a big, metal door—we would hear it slam shut by itself. Nobody really went out the back. (At the place I worked, we did haircuts, so we had a big vacuum and we only had to take the trash out once a month. So we never went out the back door; everybody took their breaks out front.) Whatever it was would slam the door.

I think the most interesting thing that happened to me there was when I went in one morning when it had snowed. In West Texas, when it snows, you don't go anywhere;

everyone stays home, because we never have snow. So it snowed one night, and I told the receptionist to close early and I would take care of things the next morning. So I came in early the next morning and locked the door and all that stuff, and then went into the back office and got to work. I heard someone laughing, and I thought, *Well, surely... maybe outside, somebody's throwing snow*, so I kind of peeked around the corner and looked, and of course there was nobody there.

It was 8:30 in the morning, and there were no footprints out in the snow or anything like that. But I'd swear the laughter was inside the shop. I just had an uneasy feeling. I did not like to be there by myself, though I never saw anything. In fact, I was so scared to be there by myself that I even had my dad come up one day when I was up there by myself, because I just always had the worst feeling there.

There were two instances when I had this strange feeling—and I don't know what it was; I've tried to actually look it up, do some research on it, and I can't figure out what happened to me, or what was going on. One night, I woke up from a sleep (and I don't remember dreaming or anything like that, and I wasn't scared), and I had a sensation of electricity. Have you ever felt when the ground conducts electricity, or has that kind of electric feel, that kind of vibration? I don't know how to explain it... It was just flowing throughout my body, throughout my whole body. The first time I had this feeling I attributed it to, you know, a deeply religious thing. I had some medical problems and stuff, and that night I prayed for God to heal me. Three years later, I woke up with the same feeling, and I don't know what it was. I have no idea. I have no clue to this day why or what.

Actually, the medical symptoms subsided once I had this feeling. I didn't go back to the doctor right away; it wasn't anything I had to be real worried about at the time, but it could have developed into something, you know? Something they had to kind of watch. And now it's years later and I don't have the problem anymore.

Candice

Texas

Chapter 22

The Shadow Knows

My wife and I joined a paranormal research group here in our small town about two years back, but I'm a bit of a skeptic. I haven't had any paranormal experiences throughout my entire life, although my wife has had a few. She's more on the believer side. You could say we're two sides of a coin. And in this particular case, we were doing more of a casual paranormal hunt, where we go with several people to a larger building or structure that had reported paranormal activity. We go in there with members of the public and we kind of escort them around and attempt to have some type of paranormal experience in the structure. The structure was here in our town, which has an automotive history, and it was an old warehouse that was used in the past, where a couple of deaths were reported.

We'd been to the warehouse, which is kind of a large, creepy building itself, many times, and did not have too many experiences ourselves, but on this particular night we were investigating with a group of six or seven of us. I don't want to call them "civilians," but they weren't necessarily paranormal investigators; they were more members of the general public just curious about what was going on in this particular building. We were on a floor where there was no electricity. Three floors up, as a matter of fact. We'd heard about some activity occurring in a particular corner of this warehouse, which was quite large. We started heading into that corner with our group, and it was very dark with flashlights turned off.

The warehouse is sort of open to the elements in some areas, and, in this particular corner, a window was broken out and casting light across the corner there. As we were approaching the corner, my wife started shouting for everybody to stop moving. I stopped and I noticed that two or three other individuals in the group were still moving, so I repeated her instructions that everybody stop moving, because I figured that she was on to something. Everybody then complied, except I saw this one particular shadow that was still in motion. And I looked at the shadow, and it was a male figure with his arm upward, raised as though he were reading something. And I thought, *Who is still moving?* The warehouse could at times be a bit dangerous...there's piles of rubble...

I thought, *Well, I've got to get this guy to stop because what my wife is saying may cause him some harm.* So I looked around the group of individuals to try to compare where people were and what position they were taking. And nobody matched the shadow. So I looked back to the shadow again—it was still there—and I looked around again, and I did that two more times. The third time I looked I started to realize the shadow had no source. And as I started to think that, the shadow moved, and took maybe two to three additional steps out of the light from the window, and then was gone. I just froze, and I started to ask, "Who else saw that?" My wife, of course, chimed in that she did, and two or three other individuals had also seen the shadow.

For the next five minutes, I went into debunking mode, and attempted to explain away the shadow. I went over to the window, and I had to almost crouch down to my knees and walk across the window frame to it. I could almost do it, if you know what I mean, but the shadow we'd seen was darker than my shadow when I simulated it. The light source that was coming in from the window was a street light that was about...oh, maybe a block and a half away, 20 feet in the air. There was no fire escape, no ledge outside the window—it was a straight drop outside a third-story window. So, it's not like somebody could have walked by.

They couldn't have walked by the light, and they couldn't have walked by the window. So that of course shook me up a little. Not "shook me up," I guess; more "excited me," if I can say that.

We started to do an EVP session kind of in the area where the shadow had moved off to. (EVP stands for Electronic Voice Phenomena, for those fellow ghost-hunters out there.) And as we started to do the session, I was facing the corner where the shadow had been. I heard a voice, kind of a mumbling, grumbling voice, off to my left, and I looked and there was a guy standing there, a part of the circle. And I asked him, "Did you say something?" and he looked at me and said, "No, I didn't say anything." And his voice, the tone and the fluctuation of his cadence was different from what I had just heard. Thankfully, by that time, I had turned on my audio recorder to catch that EVP—which was direct voice phenomena, because I actually heard it, as opposed to the electronic kind.

I have actually asked myself how this has changed my skeptical nature, if it has. If anything, I'm still very skeptical. It hasn't really shaken me to my core. It hasn't changed my world view or anything like that; I'm still very skeptical. I was expecting something like this; that's why I started paranormal investigation and research—I wanted to know if there was anything out there. Everyone was coming to me with these claims, like "I saw this" or "I heard that," so this was my opportunity to get a little bit of a taste of it, and it did kind of pique my interest, but to a large degree, I would say that I'm almost more skeptical just because I know a little bit more about what I'm looking for. So, I'm still pretty skeptical, but I qualify myself now as being among the ranks of people who have actually had an experience, even if it was a little bit on the minor side.

Jeff
Indiana

Chapter 23

A Call From Grandpa

When I was about 4 1/2 years old, back in the early '70s, my father passed away. I was pretty close to his side of the family as a child. But in the '80s, as I was growing up, life happened, and I just kind of swayed away from that side of the family.

During the early part of 1990, my grandfather (my father's father) passed away. Unfortunately, I did not go to the funeral. In August of that same year, a couple days before my birthday, I was at home in my apartment, getting ready to go to work, when the phone rang. I picked up the phone, said "Hello," and I could just hear a muffled sound. I had to say hello several times. I could tell someone was there, but I just heard a muffled sound, like the person was really really far away.

The third time I said "Hello" I heard the voice call me by name—a nickname that only my father's side of the family called me. I knew right away it was my grandfather. I knew right away. He called me "Velmita," and I really got spooked. I hung up the phone, because, I mean, I didn't understand what was going on, you know? I didn't really expect this. I hung up, and I picked up the phone again thinking I was going to get a dial tone. And he was still on the line.

I just got totally spooked. I hung up and left my apartment, because I couldn't believe it. I didn't know what to think. When I told people, I got made fun of a lot: "You got a long-distance call from heaven," blah, blah, blah. I insisted, "No. This really did happen." I know I wasn't going crazy. It really did happen.

I was 100 percent sure it was him. One-hundred percent sure. And for it to be around my birthday cinched it.

You know, I think about if I had done anything differently. It just really spooked me. I mean, going back...I don't know, I may have done the same thing. I hate to say I was frightened, but it's just something you don't expect, you know?

Velma
Texas

Chapter 24
Grandma's House

We'd just put Grandma in the nursing home, unfortunately, and we had to go clear everything out of her house, so I was going to go back and stay for a week. I took my cats with me; I was at Grandma's when no one else was there, and the cats and I would just hang out.

I think it was actually the first night that I was back there. I put away my things, went to bed—no big deal. I think at about 2 o'clock in the morning, I was sound asleep, and all of a sudden there was this huge bang. It was like someone had slammed a solid wooden door into a wooden cabinet or something. It woke me, and I was very startled.

I was sleeping in an upstairs bedroom with the door closed, and I swear that, right after that, I heard definite footsteps coming upstairs, and a tap at the door. So, I thought—and I'm trying to rationalize this somehow—I thought maybe for some reason something had happened and my mom had had to come over. So, I'm lying on the bed still, and I'm saying, "Hello?" There's no answer, and the room's still dark, and I'm like, "Okay..." I'm still trying to rationalize it...maybe I dreamed the whole thing. So I reach up and switch the light switch on, and I look down to the floor in the middle of the room, and both of my cats are staring at the door with huge eyes. So, that's when I'm like, *Okay, I didn't dream it.*

I had left my phone in another room, so I got up very carefully and opened the door, and no one was there. I got my phone and then checked the entire house, thinking maybe we'd moved something today and it fell over and I was just hearing things. Nothing. Everything was perfectly still, just where we'd left it; the doors were all locked, and there was nothing going on. Finally, when my heart rate came down to somewhere near normal, I went back upstairs, went to bed, and eventually fell asleep.

I had been lying there listening, wondering if anything else would happen. But then it sort of got odder, because nothing else happened. The next day, my mom came over to help clean things up, and when we were eating breakfast I said, "Mom, the weirdest thing happened last night." So I told her the story. She said, "You need to talk to your grandma when we get to the nursing home today." I asked, "Why?" She goes, "No, just tell your grandma the story. This will be interesting."

I'm thinking Grandma's going to laugh at me or something. We go to the nursing home, and my mom looks at her mom and says, "Mom! Robert kind of heard some stuff last night." Before I said anything, my grandma looked up and asked, "Did you hear that really loud bang, like wood slamming into wood?" And I said, "Yeah, what is that?" and she said, "I don't know, I looked, too...I've heard it a few times." And I told her everything else that happened, and she completely...she looked like, *Oh, yeah, things like that happen in the house.*

My grandma said she actually saw people in the kitchen, to the point that one day she thought that someone was in her kitchen and walked out there to see who it was, and there was no one there—no one in the bathroom right off the kitchen or anything. And she swears that somebody was walking through the kitchen.

My grandfather has passed, but that was way back in 1975, and this was just two years ago. If it were a ghost, I have no idea who this would be, actually. And, apparently— I don't like telling secondhand stories, really—but this is the house basically that my mom and her brothers grew up in. They moved there when she was in sixth grade or something, and she's the oldest. And Mom said that when they were kids, some nights they would see shadows in the bedroom. Not normal shadows. She said you'd close your eyes and hope it would go away, and open your eyes and it would still be standing there. I wasn't told any of these stories when I was a kid.

I was at this house all the time; I spent every Saturday night at Grandma's house, and nothing ever happened when I was growing up, spending Saturday nights there. That was kind of my safe haven.

What amazes me is that my grandma had heard exactly the same huge bang. It sounded like solid wood slamming into solid wood really hard.

Robert

Minnesota

Chapter 25

Man of Science Meets

the Supernatural

This happened about 16 years ago while I was working in the pathology lab in one of the major hospitals in Sydney, Australia. Working at the hospital as a scientist, you had to do an afternoon shift, in all areas of biochemistry and blood bank and so on. When you finished your afternoon shift you were generally on call, and because I live up here in the Blue Mountains, about 60 miles away from Sydney, it was easier for me to stay down at the hospital site. So if any emergency came through, they'd page you and you'd come in and do your work.

I was working an afternoon shift and I was on call, and after I finished my shift at about 11 at night I went down to the casualty section. That's called an ER in America. I went down to casualty and picked up my personal pager from the casualty switchboard and said, "I'm on call tonight." Of course, the protocol is that if something comes in, they page you. Where I was staying, well, it was a 10-story building built by someone who had absolutely no architectural merit to their name because it was this pretty blocky sort of building. I was staying on the fourth floor, and to get there... well, it was pretty involved. You had to go by service tunnel at the top, about 650 feet long, and the security people shut the whole hospital up about at 8 o'clock. So the only way to get into the building was the service tunnel. So, at the end of the shift, I went down, got my pager, logged on and said I was on call tonight, and went off to my room.

I took the stairs up to the fourth floor. But as you go up the stairs or via the lifts, you are always going to pass the security section there and they're always going to see who comes and goes. I popped my head in and said, "I'm on call tonight, I've got my pager, it's working, I'll see you later on." So I went up to my room, got changed, and went to bed. It was one of those hot and muggy nights. It was just steaming hot. I was finding it very difficult to get to sleep.

Anyway, I was nodding off to sleep for this short time and I was probably having a nightmare. And it woke me up; I was sort of woken up with a bit of a start and I turned over in the bed and looked at my watch—it was just past 1 o'clock in the morning. So I reached across to my pager to make sure it was still working and I sort of lay back in bed thinking, *I've got to be back at work by 7 tomorrow; I need to get some sleep.*

So I lay there, and the next thing I knew, I could hear footsteps coming up the stairwell. Now I just thought it very well may be someone else coming off shift and they're going off to bed as well. So I lay there and I can hear them coming up the stairwell. They get to the fourth-floor foyer and they walk down the corridor, and they walk past my door. They walk about two doors down and then I hear this sudden, loud knocking on the door two doors down, and this person calls my name out. But the interesting thing was, Jim, that they actually called, instead of them calling just "Mark," they actually called me "Mister." Which is really unheard-of because you are just known by your first name there.

The person who was in the room two doors down was a friend of mine named Alvin, who was also a med tech working the lab with me. And he's a very, very light sleeper. But this person knocked on the door and called my name out and I thought, *Well, he just got the wrong door and he should have actually paged me, so I'll just lie here until he realizes he's knocking on the wrong door and he'll come back and look for me.* So I lay there for about five minutes or so, and nothing happened. This is a bit odd. Ten minutes went past and I thought, *This is really getting strange.* So I got up and I walked down to the foyer and picked up the phone and I rang down to casualty and I said, "It's Mark here; did you send someone up for a call?" And the girl at casualty said, "No, it's been quiet since you left; nothing's come in." I said, "That's really odd, because someone's just been up here a few minutes ago looking for me. They called out and they knocked on Alvin's door but called me out and I wanna know what's going on." She said, "Well, everything's been quiet and nothing's come in. If we had something come in, we'd page you." I said, "That's right." So she said, "Why don't you try security and see what they've got going?"

So I rang security and told them the same story: "Someone's come up here the last few minutes; what's going on?" The security guy said, "We've seen no one come up past us in the last few minutes. We would've seen them or heard them. And if we needed you to be called, we'd page you." I said, "Well, I don't know what's going on here, so I'm just going to go back to bed and forget about the whole business." So that's what I did; I went back to bed and forgot about it.

The next morning, I was working in biochemistry and Alvin was working there as well. We were just chatting away and I asked, "Alvin, were you awake last night?" and he said, "Well, yeah, sort of." I said, "Just after 1 o'clock a person came up looking for me and knocked on your door and called my name out, and, in fact, they called me 'Mister.'" Alvin said, "Look, Mark, I was awake at that time and I was actually studying for my exams." He said, "I was wondering what was going on. I heard you go out and make your phone calls to casualty and to security." And he said, "I was wondering what was going on. I was going to come out and see what the matter was, but you seemed to have handled it fairly well and went back to bed." So he sort of laughed it off, saying it must've been some kind of spook or whatever, and I said "Yes, okay, fair enough."

A few days later, I was on the ward taking blood and one of the nurses came up to me and said, "Mark, we've heard about what happened to you." I said, "News travels quickly around the hospital!" She said, "Look...well, you're not the only one this has happened to." I said, "What do you mean?" She said, "Over the years, we've had medical staff who have been called out when they're on call or something in the middle of the night having someone knocking on their door and calling their name out to come to an emergency that doesn't exist." And she said, "You've got to realize, the hospital is haunted." I said, "Obviously the quarters are haunted as well." She said, "No, you're not the only one. It's happened time and time again."

Another thing too, Jim, it wouldn't have been a prank because no one would call medical staff out in the middle of the night for a joke. The first thing that would happen is they would be given their ticket and they'd be sacked. It's just amazing that when the word gets around that this happened again, the nursing staff comes back with the fact that it happened to other people, and I should just accept it.

Here is another one. I'll put you in the picture: I've been up here in the Blue Mountains for more than 25 years, and before my son was born, we had a local tragedy; we had a young child drown in one of the local dams up here, just around the corner basically. It was a tragedy; the kid had gone down to the dam on the farm and thought the water was okay and went in and drowned. A real bit of a loss there. But, just after my son was born in '87, we noticed he was getting a bit agitated and tired all the time. We couldn't work it out. But when he started talking and that, after a few years we thought, *Something is going on here.* So I asked him one morning, "Look mate, you're looking really tired; what's going on?" And he said, "Aww, there's a child that comes into my bedroom every night and all the kid wants to do is play with my toys. And the kid wants me to play with him and won't go away." And I went, "Oh, okay. Have you told the child to go away?" He said, "Yeah, I told the kid to go away because it makes me tired." I said, "Well, just put your foot down and just ignore it." But I thought, *We got a kid here who's got an overactive imagination.*

So we let it go for a while, and one night I got home from my shift at the hospital at about midnight, and the wife had dinner ready and was sitting down. We were just having our usual talk to see what was going on. We were sitting at the kitchen table and suddenly our attention was brought to the front door, and what came through the front door just flabbergasted us!

It was a bright ball of light, about the size of a squash ball, and it had the intensity of an arc welding light, but it didn't hurt your eyes. It came straight through the solid door and it stopped in the hallway and it remained there for about a second or two, not even that, and then proceeded down the hallway, and did a left-hand turn straight into my son's room. And the wife and I just went, *Okay, what is this?* Now, I've seen a ball of lightning in action, when I took physics and stuff like that, and I know what it looks like and what it can do, and this was not a ball of lightning;

it was just something completely different. Now, we weren't the only ones who actually saw it—we had an old tomcat with us at the time, and he saw it as well. And he took off after it, straight into my son's room. And the next minute, you could hear this almighty catfight going on. And the next thing we saw was the poor cat come screaming out of my son's room completely fluffed up like he had been through a tumble dry, and he just shot out through the back door, and we didn't see him for at least three days—he must have gotten hungry out in the bush! The wife and I got straight up from the table and we went straight into the room and there was nothing there. Our son was completely asleep; nothing had been stirred at all.

Over the years, while we were in that house, we kept thinking we had a fourth child in the house. I've got three kids, and every time we got them into the car, we'd always think we had a fourth kid in the back there; not three but four. The wife used to remark all the time, "There's a fourth kid." Quite often my children would say that they'd hear a pair of footsteps going up and down the hallway or someone knocking on the front door to be let in.

The interesting thing was, after we moved out of our old house to a new one around the corner here, something happened just a few years later. The wife and I were going down to do some shopping in a township about 25 miles away. She said, "Look, I'll meet you in the car; the kids are going with us." I said, "Okay, so I'll lock up the house." As I was locking up the house, I could see my wife sitting in the car, and I could see my youngest son sitting in there, iPod in his ears, listening to music and blocking out the kid sitting next to him. I locked the house up and I walked towards the car and I could still see three people sitting in the car.

So, off we drive, and as we were driving the wife was going on about how my daughter's room was so messy and how she wished she could clean it up and all that sort of stuff that teenagers generally do. And I'm sitting there going, *Okay, the wife is now chewing out my daughter who's sitting in the back being very, very quiet. Being very patient and obviously going to lose her temper here any minute.* I said to my wife, "I think you better tone things down; you're going to upset Emma. You're upsetting Emma in the back." The wife turned around and said, "What are you talking about?" I said, "You're upsetting Emma with what you're saying here and she got really quiet."

She said, "Emma's not in the back." I turned around, and sure enough, there was just Tom sitting with his headphones, his iPod, listening to his music, and that was it. I went, "I saw two people in the back of that car."

I don't know...I've always been a skeptic in many regards. Things happen for a cause or a reason or there is a reasonable explanation. But there have been times, Jim, in my life, when things have happened that completely defy any explanation. I don't know if I'm actually attracted to that or vice versa, but I think in some ways you get times in your life when those things do happen, and quite often you just completely gloss over it and don't worry about it. I think in many regards these things do happen to people, but it depends on what the circumstances are that could bring your attention to them directly and you see them as they are.

Mark
Australia

Chapter 26

Bed Shaker

I guess I was around the age of 14 when this happened. I'd been kind of admiring a set of knives that I'd acquired over the years. It had gotten late, and everybody had gone to bed. Getting ready to go to sleep, I hear something in the kitchen, so I'm thinking, *Okay, I'll be the man of the house and go check everything out*. The doors are locked and everything seems to be okay so I lie back down on the bed. The lights are out. Within a few minutes for some reason or another, I look up towards the door into my bedroom and see what looks like a figure, a silhouette of a man almost as if he's peeking into the room. I can see his head and his shoulders. And me, being young, I'm thinking, *Yeah, you* come in here! And as soon as I say it, this thing moves from the doorway to the end of my bed, the foot of the bed. And it's not as if you see him taking steps; it's almost as if it floats to the end of the bed. Being 14 or 15 years, old the first thing I do is bury my head in the covers and yell, "Arrgh!"

So after I get my head up from under the covers, I wonder what's going to happen. Then it feels like this thing, whatever it is, shakes the end of my bed. Next thing I do is, I start a-hollerin' for my mom. She's in the next room and has her door shut. She says, "It'll be just a minute." Well, I can't wait a minute. I jump up, and I run in there to tell her everything. She says, "It's just a spring in the bed," trying to ease my worries. So, I go back to the bedroom and I sit down on the bed—with the lights on, of course, thinking about what just happened, and the same thing happens again! I never heard anything like you would with a bad spring; the bed actually shakes.

I don't know if it was the same one, but I've seen this figure in the house before, and it would always be in the middle of the night. You'd see this figure; it would come into the room. It had never shaken the bed or had any kind of contact with me that I can remember.

Nick

Georgia

Chapter 27

Smoke

We live in a family home that's been in my husband's family since 1920. It was built by his immigrant grandparents and he's lived in it his whole life. I wouldn't necessarily say it's haunted, but I think that if you're a believer...maybe, some of the experiences I've had, I'd say it was more spirits or family spirits visiting, but maybe a skeptic would just write it off as something else. I would never consider it a haunting. To me, that's totally different.

The most recent "visit" has been in the last two and a half years. My husband's mother passed away, but at the time she died she wasn't living in the home and she hadn't lived in the home for four years. Nobody smokes in the house and hasn't since she lived here. Well, probably a couple of weeks after she passed away, I was outside watering the lawn and our window was open. All of a sudden I got this smell of cigarette smoke, just like how it would smell when she lived in the house. I thought, *Okay, that's truly weird.* I went in and the whole kitchen and breakfast nook area smelled as if somebody was in there and had just smoked. It wasn't smoky or anything; it just had that reminiscent kind of smell and I thought it was odd.

I went back outside and told my husband, "It smells like cigarette smoke in there and it's kind of weird." He's a skeptic and he's basically was like, "Whatever." When I went back in there 10 minutes later, it didn't have that smell at all.

For the next year or two, that kind of stuff would happen occasionally. I do think I'm more sensitive to smell—that's been my experience, and not just in this house, but other places. I assume the smell might be her, and so it got to the point where I finally said, "Hi! I know you're here, and thanks for visiting. We're doing great, but as long as you just don't show yourself that would be great." I felt kind of silly saying it, but I do not want to see a ghost. I don't mind maybe hearing something, or maybe catching a whiff of a scent, but other than that...so I've heard footsteps, stuff like that, but nothing that I would be really spooked about.

My husband, at first, his attitude was, "You're crazy; you always believe in this kind of stuff." Yet, he actually smelled it one time and he finally acknowledged that he knows what I am talking about. He thinks maybe it's something with the weather and it's coming out of the walls, so he is still a little bit skeptical, but he did smell it. His father actually passed away in the house in the late '90s, and at one point I told him I had heard him coughing down in the bedroom when I would be upstairs.

His parents' bedroom was at the foot of the stairs and he kind of blew me off about that. Not long after, he told me that he had heard it too but just didn't want to say anything. So I didn't feel that crazy after he admitted it. But it's just been very light stuff; nothing real heavy, but it's here.

Melissa
California

Part II: Of Monsters and Aliens

Ghosts, although frightening in many cases, are sort of like comfort food on our supernatural menu around the CAMPFIRE. Most of us assume, whether it is the case or not, that they represent those who have "crossed over." So, most people are a little more comfortable with them than, say, monsters or aliens.

In this part of the book, we will hear from people who experienced something quite different...and inexplicable. Buckle up—we now welcome monsters and aliens to take their seats around the CAMPFIRE.

Chapter 28

A Light That Wasn't Quite Right

When I was about 5 years old, I lived in a flat with my sister, who was about 8, and my mother. On the evening of this story, it was late at night already, about 11:30, and our mom sent us off to bed. My sister and I slept in the same room. We didn't want to go to sleep, so we sat on the bed and just talked together, while our mother was in the kitchen reading a magazine. We were looking outside the window as we talked, from our flat that was on the fourth floor. That is important for the story—it was a rather higher one, not on the bottom floor.

Suddenly we saw a bright light moving in the sky, and, in the beginning, we thought it might be a star or something like that, but it started moving in a very erratic fashion, at 90-degree turns, and it sped up and slowed down. We got really excited about it, because we didn't know what it was. After a while, it moved pretty fast, and pretty close to the window, and then it was just out of sight. Then it went out of our field of vision.

We wanted to tell our mother and ask her if she saw it as well. When we got up to go to the kitchen, a very white light came out of the kitchen, and it was like those lights you get on a soccer or football field—very, very intense; so much so that you couldn't actually look into it. It only lasted a few seconds, and then it was gone. We went into the kitchen, and our mother wasn't there, so we thought she might have gone into another room, maybe into the living room or something like that. We went there and into the other rooms, and we couldn't find her anywhere. She was just gone!

The flat didn't have anything like a trellis or anything where you could just go outside; the only way out was the main door. But it was still locked from the inside with the key in the lock, so there's no way she could have gone outside.

I didn't realize the implications, but my sister did. I was 5 years old and I didn't really start to think about the key in the lock and those kinds of things. I just thought, *Oh, Mom probably went out.*

My sister checked the door and said, "Oh, no, the key is still in the lock. It's impossible, she couldn't have gone out." We didn't really know what to do. For about an hour, we walked around in the flat, looking, searching and getting anxious—even desperate. After that, we decided to go back to bed, because at that age, more or less, that's where we felt we were safest, I suppose.

We went to bed, and that's where we must have fallen asleep, because there's nothing else I remember. We were sitting in bed and talking about where our mom could be, and the next thing I remember is waking up in bed again, still at night. I woke up more or less the same time as my sister.

The first thing we did was get up and search the flat once again. So, we went to the kitchen and our mother was there. She was sitting there again, just like we saw her before, with a magazine; reading the magazine. We were very excited, and we went towards her and asked her where she had been, and she said, "Well, I was here all the time. I only sat down a few minutes ago."

We showed her the clock and tried to prove to her that no, it had been two hours. It was about 11:30, 11:40 more or less, when we saw the light. And when we woke up again it was about 1:40, 1:45. About two hours had passed.

She couldn't account for it. She said she was still reading the same article that she started out with and to her it was as if she had sat down five minutes earlier and just started reading—that's all she remembered. She doesn't know where those hours went, where she had been, or what happened.

We have talked with my mother a few times about it since, and a strange thing that adds to the story is that when she sat down and started to read the article, she had the feeling that someone was in the room, possibly behind her, but she turned around and there was no one. So she thought, *That's strange, it's all in my head*, and she looked at the clock and began to read again. And that's also how we know more or less the exact time. She looked at the clock before she vanished.

She doesn't have any memory of what happened.

This story got me into paranormal stuff. I became more interested in it, which doesn't mean that I believe everything I hear, but I do enjoy listening to or reading stories. Our feeling is, it must have been a UFO or flying saucer of some sort and that white light must have caused her to vanish, and...I don't know, to transport her? The light came, and after that she was gone, so we think it must have been the light.

One small thing to add is that when we woke up in the morning, in daylight, we realized there were bloodstains on our bedsheets, next to our knees. But our knees didn't have any kind of injuries whatsoever, and that's something we couldn't really explain. It's like somebody tried to take blood, yet there were no marks on our knees. It is all so strange.

Marcel
Germany

Chapter 29

Spirited Away

It was the summer of 1997, and I was at my cabin in Northern Minnesota in an old, out-of-the-way town that's about 45 minutes south of the Canadian border. It is very remote, and I had very few neighbors. The closest person was maybe 10 miles away.

One night, I had fallen asleep, probably around 11 or so, and a couple of hours later I woke up. There was a very bright orange light outside my front window. And my first thought was, *My God, that's quite a bright firefly!* It was kind of bobbing up under the eaves, and I thought, *My God,* and it was just extremely bright. So then I thought, *This is not a firefly.* I kept looking at it and then suddenly I thought, *Maybe it's some kind of weird person? With a peculiar flashlight or something...I don't know.*

Well, it was bobbing around. It really looked like a giant firefly. You know how they fly and hover and bob around? That was exactly what it looked like. It stayed there. I started to get kind of unnerved, and at one point I was staring at it, thinking, *Well, maybe this is a person with some kind of strange lantern or something.* Then I remember thinking, *Oh, my God, this is not human.* Then I got really, absolutely terrified. I've never been so scared in my life.

I was by myself at the cabin, which was unusual. I was typically up there with somebody, or at least I had a dog or something with me, but this time I was completely alone. I remember just that terror, and I turned my back to the light. I turned over on my side. And I remember feeling kind of paralyzed and speechless, and that's all I remember.

It was as though I was asleep. As though I were under anesthesia—that's kind of what it felt like. You know how an anesthesiologist says, "Count backward from 10?" I think I would have reached 6 and that would have been it.

I woke up the next day at high noon. That was weird too. Okay, so I woke up, and I was lying on my back in bed, with my arms at my sides, and my eyes just popped open. Which is unusual—I usually wake up really slowly, and stretch and roll over and whatnot. But not that morning. It was really weird. I was lying flat on my back, and my eyes just popped open. I felt very refreshed; I felt okay.

I don't have any memory except the falling asleep and the fear, and then waking up the next morning at noon. It was very unnerving. I know; it's really strange. I sometimes kid around about it now, and my coworkers think I'm a lunatic, because I will tongue-in-cheek say, "Oh, I think I've been abducted." You know, by aliens. I don't know.

Emily
Southern California

Chapter 30

A Walk in the Wilderness

I've been fortunate enough in my childhood to attend a lot of camps, and I always had a great time, but there was this one time it wasn't what I would call...fun. One of the years I went, about 20 years ago, we decided to take a night hike. We were all between the ages of 15 and 18, so, old enough to take care of ourselves, but we had a counselor with us.

We were going about a half of a mile from where our campsite was. We got to walk in the woods and go up on a ridge, and go to a cave. It was really a pretty neat cave. It wasn't very big, but it was one of those that are worth finding. We decided to take a hike up there. So as we were walking up through the woods, we kept hearing these voices. They're were kind of far away, and were—I guess you'd call it—mischievous. At least, that's the best way that I can describe it. I couldn't hear what they said, and I didn't know what their intentions were, but they just kind of sounded like they were up to no good. Nothing evil, but just up to no good.

I kept thinking, *I'm hearing kids; they're being funny; they're following us through the woods. They're going to scare us because they know we're hiking.* So I was convinced that it was just that: kids—which was fine, because it wasn't frightening at that point; not a big deal. So as we were walking through, I kept hearing them, and kept asking, "Hey guys, do you hear that?" They said, "No, we don't hear what you're talking about."

So we got to the top, to our cave, and we went inside the cave. We were sitting around and talking and it was kind of cool in there, but still a nice warm summer night. We were real comfortable, but I was still hearing the voices outside. I asked again, "Hey guys, do you hear them?" And still no, "We're not hearing them; you're crazy."

So we're sitting, and talking. I kept asking and they kept saying they heard nothing. Finally I said, "Darn it, I hear something. Turn the lights on. You guys are going to hear this, or I'm going home." We turned the lights on, looked around, and one of the guys was missing. It seemed bizarre; it was like something out of a movie—it doesn't happen for real.

So it turns out he was outside the cave. His friend said, "Let me go out and talk to him; I'll figure out what's going on." He went out and talked to him and then came back in, and he said, "You know, I think we need to go." At that very moment—it was bizarre—a cold wind rushed through the cave. We all just had this feeling of fear, dread, and doom.

As a 16-year-old, it was a feeling I'd certainly never had. Just this awful feeling. We all agreed that we needed to go. So we left and went to walk home but got lost—which is strange because we had just walked up the same way. We got lost, even though it's not that big a place, and when we finally got back, and were sitting down and talking to each other, we asked each other what happened.

I was hearing voices...no one else heard them...a guy went outside...his friend has to go get him...we felt this cold wind—what really happened? As we were decompressing, we figured out that what had happened was, while we were getting into the cave and laughing, this boy was hearing the voices, too. But, unlike me, they were drawing him outside, saying, "Hey, come out and talk to us. Come out. Hey, let's do something else...hey, let's...you know, we could go hurt something; we could go kill something." Just bizarre things that didn't make any sense.

He said, "I don't know why they were telling me to do that. I didn't want to do those things, but they really wanted me to." And we asked, "Where were they?" He said, "They were down in the bushes and they kept talking to me. They kept telling me to do bad things."

So, we never figured out what it was. It's been 20 years. I'm an adult now; I look back and think it was weird. Just very strange. But I still really wonder what it was. Was it evil spirits? Were they attached to him directly? Because nobody else was affected by it. I mean, I could hear them but they didn't affect me. They didn't draw me to do anything or tempt me in any way, but I could hear them doing it to him.

As an adult, trying to deconstruct it—I guess this is me trying to be logical, but there's nothing logical about it! I get the willies thinking about it now. Right now, I have the goosebumps. And I don't tell that story very often, because it is a little bothersome to think, "I heard something I should not have heard. Something happened that should not have happened."

At the same time it makes me curious: What is it that causes something like that? Where does it come from? And the more that I look around and kind of study, the more I don't think that my experience is all that unique, necessarily. But there still really isn't any explanation.

Julie
Ohio

Chapter 31

Something's Out There!

It was 1989, I was 14, and a group of maybe 10 or 15 of us were going on a hike. It's really the only strange, paranormal-type incident I've ever had. If I could just set the stage for you here, I'll tell you about the area, so you can picture it in your mind's eye: There was this field that we were camping next to, and if you could pretend it's like a rectangle, it's about 400 yards long on the long axis and about 200 on the short. We were camping on one of the long-side axes, and it was like an old-growth type forest with a lot of evergreen-type trees. Real dark.

So that night, a group of us, about the same age, we went out to play. "Manhunt" was the name of the game. It's kind of like a group version of hide-and-seek, and we would split up into teams. My buddy B.J. and I—we remain friends to this day—decided to get on the same team. The moon was very bright; it was one of those moons that casts shadows in the middle of the night, and you don't even need a flashlight, really.

So we grouped up together as our own separate two-man team, and because of how bright the moon was, we decided to go to the long axis of the field. We thought we'd go to the other side of our campsite, on the other long side of that field, and go just inside of that tree line, where it was super dark. If you were in the field in the moonlight, you couldn't see into the wood line, but we could see out from that darkness just fine. So we were just creeping along the inside of that wood line there, and B.J., who was behind me, he heard something in the woods—leaves cracking or whatever. We stopped and listened. I didn't hear it, so we kept moving on. Then he stopped me again and swore there was something behind us, about 30, 40 yards, nothing real close...but close enough that we could make out some basic noises.

So we stopped again. We were real quiet and kept look-ing behind us. Then, sure enough, there was some type of movement coming toward us. It was just some kind of dark shape; I couldn't really make anything out and B.J. couldn't, either. Needless to say, we were freaked out, so we left the wood line and went about 20 feet into the field, looking back into the dark woods. So now we were in the moonlight and it was hard to see into this dark tree-lined edge to the boundary of the field. We were just kind of looking, and we heard something coming closer and closer. Then something stepped out briefly into the moonlight, and we only saw the head portion of it, and I estimate it was between 6 and 7 feet tall. We didn't really stay there long to get a great look, but it came out briefly, and it was only the front half of the face, if you will...it was something kind of like the face of...a cross between maybe a bear and a dog; I don't know. It was as though a bear stood up on its hind legs, but there were no noises. It didn't make any noise as far as grunting or anything like that—any animal-type noises. It briefly stepped out into the moonlight, and that's all we had to see. We turned off and sprinted as fast as we could towards our campsite, thinking there might be some older kids or adults playing a trick on us, but they were all there. There's no way anyone could have beaten us from where we saw it back to our campsite.

I hesitate to say it, but when we were in the woods, looking back at whatever was making this noise, the shape we saw did not appear as tall as whatever stepped out into the moonlight briefly.

And that's really the story. It still gives me chills just to think of it briefly coming out into the moonlight. And that's it. We didn't sleep that night; I just kept my ears open that night, listening for anything in the woods. Nothing.

It was incredible. After we got back and gathered the troops here, we walked back across the field and we didn't ever go back into those woods, but we stood out there looking with flashlights. There was never anything else that we saw or heard, and no one else did either, but I'm just glad we stepped out when we did and we heard something. I'm telling you, it was just something weird. And I still feel to this day that it was something paranormal—Bigfoot or Sasquatch or whatever—but it was unlike anything I've ever seen, from then to now. We're both 34, and B.J. and I still talk about it to this day.

Josh
New York

Chapter 32
Ol' Red Eyes

I was 11 or 12 years old, in fourth grade, and at summer camp in Florida with my Girl Scout troop. You know, with girls awake until 11 p.m. playing crazy pranks and stuff. Or so we figured. We were all getting ready for bed one night and we heard scratching that sounded like a hand on the cabin door, and we just figured it was girls being goofy. We weren't freaked out at all. Me being me, I wanted to get settled in and stop the nonsense, so I went outside and yelled, "Hey, cut it out!"

There's was no one there. So, we thought whoever it was must be hiding. We decided to just wait and see. So we turned off the lights, and about 15 minutes, later it started up again. It sounded like...not necessarily an animal, but a hand, like another girl was scratching the door. I got fed up—I felt it was ridiculous. I got up, stormed outside again, and there was nobody there. So I figured they must have dashed away, but I didn't hear any giggling or anything like that, so I went looking around the cabin.

There were a few bushes nearby, kind of in a wooded area, away from the cabins. So I went around and looked in these bushes, and there were two red, glowing dots, like eyes, looking straight at me.

I was freaked! I kind of jumped back, and hid behind the stairwell...well, not the stairwell, but there's these stairs that go up to the cabin door and are kind of elevated, so I went and hid behind there. I thought, *Maybe it was a raccoon...some kind of animal*, so I just waited. It seemed like an eternity. I was so scared, I was shaking, and being 11, everything freaks you out, so...I'd been watching for maybe five minutes when this creature, maybe 3, 3 1/2 feet tall walks out, standing on two legs like a person, and I was thinking, *What is that? Maybe a monkey or something?*

I couldn't really tell, but it looked right at me again with these red, glowing eyes, and then dashed away. I ran back into in the cabin and slammed the door, and everyone was asking, "What happened?" and I was like, "Oh my God, oh my God," you know? It was the creepiest thing. To this day, I have no idea what it was. I just can't forget those red eyes!

Melissa
Florida

Chapter 33

The Thing in the Woods

It was 1992 or '93, and I was only 16 or 17. One of my friends and I were walking home, and we decided to take a shortcut through this trail that we always go through. It was probably between 8:30 and 9 o'clock at night. We were walking through the trail and I was leading the way, and... well, it was really dark and I couldn't see, so I ended up getting us off the trail. We went off into the woods, probably about 20 yards or so before my friend noticed that we were off the path. He started leading us back and we finally got back onto it. As soon as we did, I felt a gust of wind go behind me, and there was no wind blowing at all. I thought it was kind of strange, but we didn't really think much about it. As soon as that happened, we started walking and we heard tiptoes in the bushes.

We'd take four or five steps and then the tiptoeing would catch up to us. So that's when we started thinking that something was going on, but we weren't really taking it seriously. It sounded like a little rabbit or a cat, so we thought maybe a little animal was following us. My friend was joked about how it might be a wolf or whatever, and he was playing like he was going to take off running, and as soon as he did that, that's when it started happening: There was a little ball of light going along on the ground, probably about an inch off the ground. And first it was like a little ball—you know those fireworks, they call them jumping jacks, and they kind of bounce around? The difference was that it was going straight, going alongside us, not all crazy like the fireworks. All of a sudden, you could start to see the form of the thing inside of the ball; it looked sort of like a little rat that was standing up on its hind legs, walking. It was like that. Then, all of a sudden—I mean, this all happened in a few seconds—it started to get bigger, in an instant. And it got anywhere between 10 feet and 15 feet tall. And it was made out of...it didn't have skin like me and you. It was...the only thing I can describe it would be ether.

I have heard similar stories since. A guy I went to school with said it happened to him probably about two years after that. He said he tried to run from it, and when he tried to run from it it broke down into shadows of some type and attacked him. He ended up going to the hospital.

The thing was very strange. It looked a lot like the Predator, from the movie. It had dreadlocks on its head and spikes all the way down its back. And it was hot...it was like standing next to a stove with the door open, you know?

I don't have any further information on it. I've been trying to find something...thinking maybe somebody had drawn something that was similar to it, but I haven't found anything close to what it really looked like.

Tim

Nevada

Chapter 34

Out-of-Body Visitors

One morning, when I was 18, I believe, I woke up and went to use the little ladies' room. Across the hallway into the parlor I saw my dog sleeping on the couch. My dad had just gone to work and he would've yelled at her if he'd seen her on there, but I didn't. *Go ahead and sleep*, I thought. *I won't bother you*. I went over and I gave her a big hug. As I hugged the dog, it seemed I was instantly seeing myself from the ceiling area of the living room.

It was an out-of-body experience. It's interesting that, as I saw myself, I wasn't afraid at all. I just remember thinking, *Well, this is weird*, you know. Anyway, I was up there looking down at myself, not thinking too much about it, I guess, and then I looked over into the kitchen. Again, I was looking down from the ceiling. I looked over and I saw a man, a very three-dimensional dark shadow of a man wearing a wide-brim hat and a long coat of some sort, just standing there, looking at me sitting on the couch in the living room.

I'm not even sure if I believe in possession or not, but the first thing I thought of when I noticed that he was looking at me was *Oh my God, I'm not in there. Maybe he could get into my body*.

Before then, there had been no supernatural activity in the house. That was really the first thing that ever happened. From the angle of his hat, I could tell he was looking at me, and it scared me and I gasped. When I gasped, I was instantly back in my body again, on the couch, looking into the kitchen where I had seen him, and the dog was looking there too. I wasn't scared, but I didn't want to be in the parlor anymore.

It is understandable that some people think it was a dream. I'd probably think the same thing if I was hearing the story and it didn't happen to me. The only thing I can say is that I know I was awake, because I woke up and walked out there. You know, I slept well. It's not like it was really late at night or I hadn't rested for an extended period of time.

After that, there was something else that happened in the same home that was very strange. Hopefully most people hearing this won't think I'm half a lunatic! I think I'd be questioning if I heard this. What happened this time was probably several months later. This was later at night, maybe around 10 o'clock, and my dad was asleep in the back room. I was on the phone. I walked from my room to the bathroom, again, and looked across the parlor (because the way the house went, there's my room, and across the hall there's a bathroom, but to your left if you look across there's the parlor, and the kitchen after that, and a big mirror on the far wall of the kitchen). So, as I was walking, I glanced into the mirror, being a typical vain teenage girl, and I saw in the room behind me what I can only describe as a gray alien head, only the ears I remember being pointed like Spock or something.

I didn't hear any voices or anything like that; I just got the feeling that the thing was probably just as shocked as I was, because when I just saw its head it wasn't looking at me. It was looking straight ahead the other way, so I was seeing it from the side. I gasped and looked away. I looked back, thinking, *It's not going to be there, this is too outrageous, this can't be happening.* As I turned my head and looked back it was still sitting there, and it turned its head and looked at me. When it did, I just got this feeling...

I'll never forget those black eyes. They were just black as black, but I just got the feeling that it was in shock that I was there looking at it. It left me with a lot of questions and I don't know that I'll ever have the answers.

Jennifer
Montana

Chapter 35

The Night Visitor

It's a little hard to start with this. I haven't told too many people.

Probably when I was about 20 years old, I went to bed one night and I remember waking in the middle of the night. I had a sense or a feeling that there were beings or entities around me, and the strange thing was actually that I was awake, but I wasn't in my room. The other thing was, I was pretty much immobile. I couldn't move from the bed. The only light normally in the room when I slept was a blue alarm clock. But now I saw light coming through the window. It was also blue but an encompassing light—that's really the best I can say.

In particular, I remember one being that was standing over me, and he had—I say "he" but I'm not really sure what it was, because it looked like it wore a dark cloak, I guess you could say. But out of his dark cloak he had his finger pressed on my forehead, and that is actually what I felt, what was holding me down. Honestly, I was terrified. All I wanted to do was just scream and get out of there. This thing was holding me down with its finger, and it was kind of a long, very cold finger, and I remember a single black fingernail.

Since this experience it's been about 12 years, and I've had some things happen to me, and I've almost made peace with it. I've heard some other people tell their stories on THE CAMPFIRE, and I kind of hope that someone might hear this and shed some light on it. And, too, I've been thinking, soul-searching about this particular instance, and I kind of have a theory of my own. But if I may just kind of get back to that place...

At the time this happened—if I can paint the picture a little better—at the time I was 20 years old, and I lived with my father and my brother, and I was on the second floor of a Cape Cod–style home. My brother was asleep in the bedroom across the hall. And, like I said, when this happened I was asleep; I did wake up and I distinguished the outline of this figure standing over me. As it came closer to put its finger on my forehead, I could see its face, and it was very humanoid-looking, with larger eyes that I would describe as black. I couldn't really detect a pupil. Just deep, black, soulless eyes. And it was staring at me and had its finger on my forehead. And as this was happening I had a sense of other beings around me.

This is going to sound weird, but the bed I was lying on... it felt like a different bed. It was cold; it was hard. I had blue sheets on my mattress, but the sheets that were actually on me were black. I know that's a weird detail to remember, but I did. I remembered it.

I had the sense that my body had been transported elsewhere by whatever means. To be honest with you, I can't get past the cover of that famous book *Communion*. Which is kind of funny. But, see, about the cover of that book, it's close to what I saw that night, but it's not quite right. I mean, it was pale, but this thing that I saw, its face was pale, but it wasn't the gray alien that he described. It was pale, and it was humanoid-looking, but it had no expression; no emotion. It wasn't friendly, and I got the sense of no feeling or no emotion.

I was physically terrified at this point, I have to tell you. I have suffered in the past from night terrors, which you'd probably say is the old-hag syndrome, but this was a totally different experience. With this, I was awake. And at the conclusion of this, I got a feeling of whatever was around me, whatever beings were around me, doing what they were doing...they went away, and the last thing was this one taller being in this dark cloak, still staring at me with the blue light that just encompassed me...he basically started backing away into the light, and he took his finger off my forehead, and that's when I noticed the black fingernail. As it started disappearing into the blue light, I remember seeing its pale face kind of disappear into the black cloak, and once that happened, I was back in the darkness of my normal room.

At that point I literally jumped out of my bed. My brother can confirm this—I ran into the door so hard that I actually put a crack in the wooden door with my shoulder. I was fumbling for the handle; I couldn't get out of the room, and I remember him turning on the hallway light and opening the door, and he kind of looked at me, scared but kind of laughing, and he asked me what I was doing. And I looked at him and I couldn't say anything other than that I had no idea.

I've had experiences since then, but nothing like this one. That was probably the worst case of it, and the most frightening. It might even have been the first time. But it seems like what is going on is more like a telepathy or something. (And this isn't only my opinion; I've done some readings, I've heard some other podcasts, and even your show.)

The most recent experience I've had was just a month or two ago, and it's actually what prompted me to respond to the show...

I was sleeping in bed with my wife, lying on my side looking at the side of the room and dreaming of what was essentially the head of this gray alien, kind of walking in the room towards me. The room is bright white. I know I'm dreaming, and I want to get out of my dream. I'm kind of scared, but it starts smiling at me and puts up its hand to wave, which is very, very weird. Then the light explodes and I want to wake up, but I'm having sleep paralysis. I roll over onto my back, I scream, and I open my eyes, and above my eyes there's—what do you call them? An orange ball of energy kind of floating over my head. And as I start to wake up, it dissipates, the little molecules of energy dissipate, and my wife put her hand on my shoulder and asked me what was wrong. And again I couldn't really tell her. I couldn't even describe it. But again, whatever was going on, it wasn't in the room with me. Maybe I saw an energy or had an energy or a presence in the room, and it was maybe communicating telepathically, I don't know.

Shane
New Jersey

Part III: Tales of Dreams and Death

Few experiences impact a person more than a communication with a deceased loved one or a supernatural event surrounding a death. I should know, because the former happened to me. (But more on that later.)

Another area we delve into at times on the CAMPFIRE is that of strange dreams, either those that put us in touch with the "other side" or foretell some future doom. Even if they are Scrooge's "undigested gruel," these dreams have a way in getting inside our heads—where they tend to take up permanent residence.

Has anything like this happened to you? Have you found yourself dreaming of or talking to dead relatives lately? Whether yea or nay, these experiences make for great stories. Let's take our seats back around the CAMPFIRE to hear about some of these life-changing events.

Chapter 36

Love Is Like a Butterfly

My story is about my grandfather.

In the summer of 1997, I was working for my parents. They owned a car lot, and my job was to check the cars in the morning to make sure there was no vandalism or anything, and make sure everything was locked up.

I was making my rounds one morning, and I came across a tiger butterfly on the concrete, on the lot, and it was dead. It was perfectly preserved and beautiful—not damaged or anything. Now, I've always been kind of a cynic and I'm not a big crier. But I picked it up, and I just had this well of emotion come over me. I went into the office with my mom, showed her the butterfly, and I just couldn't stop crying. It was just so absurd...you don't cry over a dead butterfly. My mom was very understanding about my reaction, but she didn't understand it, either.

A few minutes later the phone rang, and it was my grandmother saying that the ambulance was coming to pick Papa up because he thought that he was dying. This was not the first time that he'd had that fear (Papa had had lung cancer for several years at that point). You know. Cancer—it's so hard on the body.

I asked, "Should I go with you to the hospital?" She said, "No, stay here at the lot; I'll call you if I need you to come up there." I said okay. She went on up to the hospital and I stayed.

It wasn't long. Probably after about...oh, 45 minutes or so, she called and said, "You need to come on up here." So, I locked the car lot up real fast—I don't think I'd set the alarm; I just locked up and ran. It was a small town, and there weren't a whole lot of stoplights, but I think I ran every single one to get to the hospital.

When I got there, my uncle told me to go on back to Papa's room, so I did, and I got there just in time to see him take his last breath.

I know that I screamed something when the doctor said that he was gone. I just...I didn't want to let him go.

Anyway, after he passed, we all went back to my grandmother's house and already there was sweet tea and chicken and people were bringing stuff over. But I had this feeling...I just needed to get away. I couldn't...I wasn't hungry; I just needed some space.

So I went for a drive in the country, kind of aimlessly. And while I was driving, I saw a little pond alongside the road. I pulled over, got out, and just sat by the pond. I could never find this place again; it was just one of those places by the road. I was just sitting there and this huge swarm of tiger butterflies was everywhere. There were 20 or 30 of them. They were in my hair, they were on my shoulders, they were on the grass at my feet, they were by the pond... they were everywhere.

Usually when you see them, they might be passing by on the breeze as they migrate on, but all of a sudden, I was surrounded by them, and they were in my hair and on my shoulder, and then they just took off. It was just...just magical. In that situation, you just kind of sit there and think, *Did that really happen?* It was so fast...but it felt like forever when they were touching me, and then they were gone. To this day—and I told my mother this story, and it's kind of a bond we have now—if I'm having a bad day, or if my mother's having a bad day, a little tiger butterfly, or a little yellow butterfly will go by, on a day that you need to see it. I kid you not, it could be the dead of winter, when there's no bud anywhere outside. It is just the most bizarre thing in the world. That day, Papa was communicating with me. I believe that; I honestly do. I'll always believe that.

Beth
North Carolina

Chapter 37

A Vision of Uncle Charlie

When I was growing up, I didn't have my grandparents, but we had a close family friend that I kind of adopted as my grandparent. He was older and would spend time with our family, and we became close. Probably a little closer than I thought. (As I tell the story you'll see why.) I always called him Uncle Charlie. One night, when I was around 11, I went to bed, and had a very odd dream, one that was so striking that I woke up the next morning and told my mother about it.

It was strange, and very vivid. I still remember it today, and I'm in my 40s. The dream was in a sepia tone, which (for people who don't know what that is) is sort of brown and white. Almost like an old movie.

The dream was set in what appeared to be a dungeon of some type with stone walls and a stone slab, and a person was lying on the slab. There were four or five people shorter in height than what I would consider normal-sized, all wearing white. They surrounded the stone slab and then started to actually pound the chest of the person who was on the stone slab. I got a look at the person on the stone slab and it was Uncle Charlie. I probably remember five or eight minutes of the dream very vividly, but that was the core. The crux of the dream was the constant pounding on this person's chest in the dream, and these smaller people scurrying around and doing this action over and over and over again. Finally, a white sheet that was on my Uncle Charlie was pulled completely over him.

There were no religious icons during the dream. It kind of played out in my mind as an old-fashioned movie, so that was weird. There were torches on the wall almost like an old Frankenstein-type movie. It was strange.

The next morning, my mother and I were sitting around the table having breakfast, and I told her the story. She looked me in the eye and told me that before I had gotten up, she had received a phone call that my Uncle Charlie had died that evening, while I was asleep. He had had a heart attack, and they tried to revive him using all sorts of measures that have something to do with resuscitating and pounding—all the things I had seen. What I saw was pretty convoluted compared to what actually happened. I'm guessing that Uncle Charlie was actually thinking of me, maybe, during this process, and projected it into my head, into my dream, so I kind of saw what was happening. What I saw was almost in a different form of reality, but it was what was happening. I saw it almost like an old-fashioned movie, and it still haunts me to this day. Not in a bad way, but it was so vivid. It was probably one of the most vivid dreams I've had in my life, and I was dreaming it the same time that he was dying.

My initial reaction after my mother told me he'd died was just one of being freaked out, not knowing why I would have those images. I guess my mother was the one who immediately comforted me by telling me that it was probably a good thing: In a way, it was my Uncle Charlie's way of showing how close I was to him. I viewed him as a grandfather; he may have viewed me as a grandson figure. I guess in a way, my mother was at least trying to comfort me by telling me that his last thoughts on this earth were thoughts of me, and somehow it got passed along to me.

I was freaked out in the beginning of the dream, but it wasn't a scary situation; there was no blood or gore or anything like that. It was more the images of him trying to be revived. So I guess I've always looked at it as a positive image. I haven't had an experience like that since, so I don't know why it happened. I'm only speculating that we were on the same wavelength for that short period of time that evening.

I wish I'd have other experiences like it, so I'd have something to which to compare it. Maybe I'll never have another like it again, but the way I look at it is that, for those two or three minutes, that vivid part of the dream that stuck in my head (and is still stuck there), there was some sort of connection going on, between someone who was dying and someone who was close to him, which was me. And I can't explain it any other way...I wish I could. I wish I knew. It's an experience that I'll always remember. Regardless, I know that it's valid and true.

Rich

Massachusetts

Chapter 38

Mom's Deathbed

When my mom was in her 80s, she took ill from multiple strokes. We took care of her for quite a few years. She had a great sense of humor, and was a wonderful person. Eventually, though, she deteriorated to the point where we had to put her into a hospital down the street. Then one evening, we got the call that her oxygen level had dropped to 65 percent, and the whole family rushed to her bedside.

We surrounded her and the doctor basically said, "She's gone." It was time for her to pass. So I was holding her hand,

and my brother was with her, too. He was a fire chief and an EMT, and he was being very analytical, holding on to her wrist and listening to her pulse. As she was passing away, she shed a single teardrop...

I've got to say real quick: I've never seen a ghost. I'm not even sure if I believe in them.

So, I'm watching my mom, and the teardrop is almost like a third eye. I could see something happening right in front of me, right by her chest, and I could hear a whooshing sound. As the tear dropped from her cheek, this brown swirl just came out of her, and within a second it crossed the distance between us, and hit me—thump—right in the chest. Then it was gone. Right at that point my brother said, "She's gone." I said, "No...no, no, no, no, no...she's not gone."

Now, I didn't feel possessed or anything like that, and the feeling faded away, but it was the most amazing thing for me. I saw this brown swirl just float right from her to me as she passed away.

This happened about 10 years ago, and I think what it really meant to me is that we're more than just this physical body. Maybe we travel from body to body. It kind of got me wondering, really, what kind of creatures we are. Are we something like an energy force that we imprint upon, that we get imprinted upon, and we move from being to experience to experience?

My father passed away two years later, and I wondered if this was going to happen again. Thank God, I was fortunate to be with both of my parents when they passed. With my dad it was just a quieting of the room, as if he just left. There was nothing there. So I don't really understand what happened with my mom. I've never seen a ghost; I've never seen anything like this before, and I have never heard of a story like this. While we were all there awake, I was the only one who saw it. My mom and I were very, very close. To see this...almost like a swirling gas come at me, it was kind of a shock, as you can imagine.

Steph

Massachusetts

Chapter 39

A Pat on the Shoulder

I work in a factory as a welder. The day after my father's funeral, I was welding at my bench, and my back was about a foot away from the wall. I had my welding helmet down and I was welding away, and I felt a pressure on my left shoulder. Someone or something squeezed my shoulder—it was as if someone was standing behind me, and just gave me a gentle squeeze. But there was no one behind me. It was an actual pressure that came on and went off, just as if someone was standing behind me, giving me a reassuring little touch.

It was very, very weird. I instantly stopped welding, took off my helmet, and turned around just to make sure that no one had sneaked up behind me. But there was no way someone could have gotten behind me, because there was a brick wall there. So...again, it was very strange.

My father's death was a surprise, but he had been ill with heart trouble. He died of a heart attack in the hospital—before we could get there, actually. I had to pick up my brother from another part of town, and we raced down the motorway, going through many, many red lights and speed cameras. We got there, but it was too late.

That day in the factory, it was as if he was just saying goodbye, really; letting us know that everything's okay. It was very, very strange—a definite feeling, like someone squeezing the shoulder and letting go...a brick wall right behind me...very weird.

David
United Kingdom

Chapter 40

Dad's Last Goodbye

My father passed away when I was about 17. I remember a few days after his passing having an amazing dream. I remember it because it felt like no dream I'd ever experienced before. It was so vivid that I can remember every detail of it. It just felt more like a real experience, a wide-awake experience, than any dream.

In my dream, I woke up early in the morning, before the sun even came up. My bedroom was up on the second floor and the stairs that led down into the kitchen were right outside my bedroom door. I remember I woke up and I heard noises down in the kitchen—the sounds of things being moved around, cupboards being opened and closed—and I was thinking to myself, *That's really odd, because nobody usually wakes up this early in my house*. So I went downstairs to investigate, and as soon as I turned the corner into the kitchen, there was my father standing in the kitchen, and he was looking up at me, and there was this little bit of a smirk on his face, and I remember I was just looking at him in shock.

I said, "Dad, how can you be here? You died just a few days ago and I was at your funeral." He was just looking at me and just nodding. He was standing there in front of me, exactly how I remembered him, exactly how he used to... the same clothes he used to wear, the same flannel shirt, just making himself a cup of coffee in the kitchen. And he basically said to me, "I just wanted to come and see you one last time, and let you know that I'm good. Everything is fine with me. You don't ever have to be sad for me; I feel fine; I'm great; everything's good, and I just wanted to stop by and say that to you and see you one last time."

Right after that, I woke up—for real this time—and I sat up in my bed. I was completely shaking. All I could think was, *Wow. That was amazing.* So I shared that with my girlfriend, who is my wife now. It was amazing and all, but the weird thing about it came later on in the year, during Thanksgiving dinner. After the meal was finished, my family was sitting around the table, and we were talking about different things, and the subject of the paranormal came up, and it made me think of my dream.

I shared my dream with the rest of my family, and one of my brothers was looking at me and I could see his jaw drop. After I finished my story, he said, "I had the same exact type of dream." He described it exactly the same way. It was the most vivid, wide-awake experience of a dream that he ever felt, except there was a little bit of a twist, because it wasn't as pleasant as my dream was. Basically, the way his dream was, apparently our father woke him up out of bed. You see, after my father had passed, my brother became very depressed, and he'd started drinking heavily. And so in his dream, my father was there, woke him up, and was yelling at him and said, "Listen, you better straighten up your life; you'd better turn this around. I want you to stop with this drinking. You have to be strong; you have to take care of your mother!" Basically, he was yelling at him to straighten out his life. Well, it really shook him up and he really did turn everything around. And I guess that made my father happy.

Oh, it made me a complete believer in the afterlife, and...you know, I really believe that it wasn't just a dream. I really believe that he did visit me from beyond the grave. I think he did it to leave a message that there is life after death and, you know, it's a good thing.

Tom

New Jersey

Chapter 41

Strange Dreams of Buildings and Planes

It was the strangest dream I'd ever had. Well, it seemed like it was more than just a dream, because it was so vivid and very symbolic. And it was a two-part dream. Once I fell out of one dream, I fell into another.

In my dream, I was looking across the horizon and there was almost like a row of buildings or a tall building—but not real tall; probably about the height of the Pentagon, I guess, from my view—and an airplane that was flying (and I didn't understand it; it looked just like a regular passenger airplane) suddenly nose-dived down towards the building, and then there was this huge explosion. Out of the explosion, there was this blue flame...I didn't understand that either.

Suddenly, there was a movie playing inside of the explosion, like a slideshow of imagery, one thing after the other. It was too hard to even take in, at the time. I wish I could have remembered everything, but none of it made sense at the time. 9/11 hadn't happened yet.

I went to work the next day, and I was very vocal about it. I said, "I know we're going to be attacked on our soil; it'll be the first time for that. It'll be devastating. Life will not be the same afterward for us."

One weird thing about the dream, too, was that I was standing outside of a company I used to work for, and that's the road I was looking across when it happened. After it happened, I had a strange feeling come over me...chills... kind of like I saw a ghost or something. I looked up at the sky, and I looked up for about 15 minutes—what seemed like 15 minutes—just looking and looking, and there were no airplanes in the air. And I just remember at the time it came over me like a heavy weight. When I got to work I said, "There will be no airplanes in the air. They will just not be there." And that was an interesting coincidence, too; for the first time ever, our government said, *Let's institute a no-fly zone over the entire United States*. That's not something you just come up with out of the blue.

This dream occurred about six months before 9/11. After it actually happened in real life, and I pieced it together, I couldn't believe it. *Wow! I dreamed this kind of stuff would happen*. I almost feel that I should have gone and had somebody hypnotize me and reconstruct this and put it all together. Because I know there are pieces of it that are there, but if I try to remember them, sometimes I think that I may just be making them up in my mind. I tell myself that. But if I could remember that slideshow, that would be interesting. I remember some sort-of symbolic stuff in it, but I can't really grasp a lot of it.

But then the second part of it that was rolled in was rather interesting, because it was like all of a sudden I wanted to hold on to what was going on here. I fell into this other dream, the second part, where everything was not black-and-white, but almost a sepia with lots of sand, and I saw big cement walls that were partial walls, and I couldn't understand it. I wondered, *What the heck is this?*

Then I saw my brother with other military guys, and at some point he had his helmet off, which I thought was weird. They were running from and trying to escape from some attack that was coming. There were bouncing bombs, or something was popping up from the sand. I didn't understand that. Then there was a sudden understanding that my brother got shot.

I tried to hold on to that and I thought, *I've got to try to find out what's going on here.* That's when I woke up. Later, this too ended up happening: My brother got shot in the arm while in active duty during the war. His group was escaping an enemy attack over there. I believe he was rescuing his lieutenant, and he got shot in the arm. Another guy got shot too, but they both survived. And my brother was real lucky; they said the bullet missed all the important stuff. A happy ending on that part. Of course, I didn't tell my mom about the dream about my brother until after it was all over. Luckily, my brother has recovered and is doing well. One last thought: maybe the reason I had a premonition regarding the Pentagon and not the towers was because I'm related to somebody who was connected with the Pentagon—my brother.

Mark
Illinois

Chapter 42

Granddad Watches Over Her

First of all I have to say that my daughter has many abilities.

Her granddad passed away about four years ago when she was 5 years old. At the time, she had come to me or my husband several times in the early morning hour, and would ask us if we were calling her. We would say no, and finally she figured out that her granddad was calling her. We asked her how she knew it was him, and she made several references to things that only he would know—not things that he would tell a 5-year-old, but things he would say to identify himself for my mother-in-law's sake, if that makes any sense...I know it's very hard to follow.

He would call her name, and he'd say to her that he's okay. He would really reassure her, and come to her in dreams. Yet the dreams were so intense that she would think his visits happened while she was awake. She was also able to visualize him. She would see things that he would wear, and she would describe them to my mother in law, and that is how she was able to identify him.

I have to be honest: I was really a disbeliever. Still, I wouldn't do anything to discourage my daughter at that age, because I felt that that was her way of mourning. Maybe it was her way of dealing with things.

However, my mother in law had started to notice that when my daughter would show up to the house, certain things would occur, such as electrical disturbances in the home. If my daughter were to spend the evening, certain things would turn on in the house without anyone touching them. A lamp would go on, or a calculator would go on, or things started to go on that wouldn't normally go on. Like a ceiling fan.

My mother-in-law shared this experience with me. I thanked her, but again, I felt that that was their way of mourning; I did not believe it was real. But then something happened that changed my mind. My daughter was very sick with a flu virus. It was very serious, and she had a high fever. It was so high I was considering taking her to the emergency room or calling 911. I wasn't really sure what to do. She was non-responsive and kind of lethargic, and it was scaring me. Then she fell into a very deep sleep, and I put my hand on her head and felt that she seemed to be cooling down. So I stepped back and I sat on a chair where I could see her face. I was watching her as I was reading a book, and I got up several times to read her temperature by touch. Again, it seemed to be fine. Not that she didn't have a temperature, but it wasn't as high as it had been.

I should say that the room had a general feeling of heaviness at the time. It is very hard to explain, but it was just a heavy feeling...

I looked at my daughter, and she started to nod her head. As she nodded, I then realized that I was sensing something. Something was going on, and it was not normal. It was very heavy around me. And so I said, "Lee," which is the name of her granddad, "I know that you're here, and if you're here, let me know if she's okay." Just then, the ceiling fan instantly turned on. The hair on my arms stood up, and I wasn't fearful, but I was definitely aware; mainly because of the heaviness, I knew that something was going on.

There's one more part of the story that solidifies it. As I was sitting across the room and my daughter began to nod her head yes, I went down to my knees next to her and I held her hand. She opened her eyes, and had a very large smile on her face. She said, "Mom, I just saw Granddad!" I told her, "I know you did." She said, "He told me that he loved me."

Of course, I was completely taken aback. It certainly made a believer out of me. After that night, I couldn't deny it.

Christina
Arizona

Chapter 43

A Vision Before Living

Ever since I was 7 or 8 years old, I could remember a certain place that I had visited. No one else I know has had a similar journey. What is extremely remarkable is when I visited it: before I was born.

I can only explain this place as another dimension or a different plane. I recall dying in a previous life and suddenly finding myself in a very dark place. I can't recall anything of that past life itself, but I remember the time between lives with a lot of detail. There, in this place, I received the knowledge and understanding of how and why life works the way it does.

While I was in the dark place after my past-life death, I started thinking, *Death is nothing but a transition*. Of course, you feel sorry because you have to leave the people that you have lived with here, but at the same time, there's a warm and a loving feeling that surrounds you.

As these things were taking place, I saw a guide. I recollect it as a Being of Light. It was an angel, or...I don't know what it really was, but he wasn't very talkative. I would ask him, "Are you my grandfather?" He wouldn't respond. "Are you a friend of mine?" No response.

Then from the dark place I was being pulled through, at great speed, a tunnel made of light—millions of lights everywhere. Suddenly, it stopped. I found myself in front of a figure. The Being of Light was emitting this whitish glow, but now there was an additional figure, this one more bluish.

Because of the understanding you receive when you're on the other side, I immediately knew who this figure was. It was Jesus. He wasn't very talkative, either, and I was in shock, as you can imagine. Because Jesus was actually in front of me and alive, I thought, *He's got to be the son of God, or, if he's not, somebody very special.*

He had a long robe. I don't want to influence people and/or have them say that I am trying to guide them into Christianity or Catholicism. I don't mean to do that because I have enough to deal with concerning my own burden, as I will explain, than to worry about what people are going to think.

The Being of Light was there with Jesus and me—it was just the three of us. Everything else was pure darkness. The Being of Light seemed to move further back, so I was positioned closer to Jesus, and then right in front of him this screen popped up. I can only explain it as a holographic screen. Then, I started seeing my life review.

I started looking down immediately, asking for forgiveness, so I didn't really see much of the review. There's got to be a reason for that, I guess. I was very much in shock, and I thought, *Okay, if he's Jesus and death is not the end, then I guess I'm going to be sent to Hell right now.*

When my life review was over, Jesus started talking to this Being of Light, or angel. He approached Jesus and there was some communication between them that I could not hear. I'd describe it as telepathic. But, I didn't have access to it. Then the Being of Light started hovering towards me.

I thought, *He's the one who's going to take me to Hell.* We began traveling to this other place, but I looked back, and I asked Jesus, "Do I get another chance? Do I get to live again? Or is this it?" He didn't answer, and suddenly I was in this dark void, alone. I was just pacing around in circles, floating in this emptiness, alone with my thoughts.

Maybe I should have been a priest in my past life? Maybe I should have led a more holy life? It was very confusing. *Maybe this was Hell? Perhaps I'm a soul now and cannot die.* Being alone there forever was a pretty scary thought. So, eventually I looked up, and I yelled "Father!" and then instantly the Being of Light showed up and I was brought in front of Jesus again. I don't know how long I stayed in the dark void. It felt like 10 minutes, but it could have been a hundred years. Time in that place doesn't apply like it does here in the physical world.

At that point, the knowledge that I had to pick what I wanted to be in my next life was revealed to me. I was going to be reincarnated, I guessed. I was still in shock because of the whole process.

I asked him, "Is man dying and reincarnating forever?" Then, and this was the only time he answered me, I was told that there's not much more time left for man.

Suddenly, I felt an urge to pick what I wanted to be in my next life. I was shown the concept of different careers in general terms—what it is to be a doctor, or a fireman, etc. For example, I was shown what it was like to play guitar, and I loved it. So I asked, "Can I learn how to play guitar?" And, I was given that information, that knowledge—how to play guitar. I explained that I was not ready to be a priest or anything like that, but that I would like to be, at least, a good person. He didn't answer, but I was filled with information, with knowledge. I just felt it was telepathic. Then, I saw what it was like to draw and paint. I loved it. So I asked again, "Can I learn how to do those things?" And again I was imparted those skills. After saying I wanted to know how to play guitar and how to draw, this holographic screen popped up again in front of me. As I was looking at it, I could see that these talents were going to be a large part of my future life. Since I was a kid, I've been a natural talent at playing guitar—nobody taught me.

I also saw that I was going to learn English. I knew that I was going to live in a foreign country other than Spain where I was born. I'm here now in the States. I saw many different things. I saw old buildings, which I later recognized when I drove around Austin after moving here. I recognized the architecture.

Here's what changed my mind on telling people about my experience: I kept seeing different visions, but one of the most disturbing was when I reached my 30s. I was shown that I would develop some kind of pain in my legs and my arms. At that point, I received the knowledge, automatically, that this was the beginning of my end for me. I got concerned, so I asked, "Can you remove this from my fate? You know, get rid of it?" and then he looked away and I saw a negation. He just looked away, meaning that it was indeed going to be my fate. As we went on, I saw a preview of myself telling my sister and my mother and my father in this life about my pre-life experience, and it was made clear it would be at Christmastime.

I have had a strong validation of the vision. This very thing happened in real life. I went back to Spain this past Christmas season and told my family about this memory. Until recently, I have always assumed this "experience" was just a dream, so it's not a self-fulfilling prophecy, as I'm sure some people will say. A year ago, I started getting tremors in my arms, and then that developed into pain that I still have today. Right then, I thought, *Wow, hold on a second. I'm in my 30s, and I have this kind of pain in my legs and my arms...*

I've seen doctors for the condition, and that's something I asked Jesus about as well. I asked, "Can doctors help me?" He looked away again, saying no, telepathically. After that I asked him, "Could you please give me a wife who can help me through the process and be of support?" Right then, I saw my wife, exactly what she would look like. I immediately knew it was her. She's from America, but we met in Spain. I said, "She's beautiful, Father, thank you." She is helping me through my situation today, just as I had asked.

So, here I am, with this condition and this experience. What can I do with this information? People might think I'm crazy but I've decided to tell my story, because it has some very interesting things in it. I thought the story should be told and that it might help others.

Francis

Texas

Chapter 44

The Dream of a Funeral

Before I start, I have to say that I'm a big skeptic. I don't believe in stuff easily, and I only believe in this premonition because of how it happened. Otherwise, I wouldn't have believed it at all.

Six years ago, I lived near my grandma, and one weekend we planned a trip for Sunday. I wanted to go to a nice little town, but the day before we planned to go, I had a really weird dream. I dreamed of a burial. I didn't know who it was. In the dream, I was just crying and crying. There was a casket in the middle, but I didn't know who it was. I woke up in tears, and I said, "Oh, what a weird dream!" I didn't even think that it could have been a premonition.

We went on the trip, and when my dad was taking a turn in the car, it kind of fishtailed, and we crashed straight into a police truck.

My grandma died that night. It was a long time ago. I told my family a year afterward that I had had a premonition, and my mom said, "Come on, you should have told me! I believe in that!" I said, "I usually don't." But you know, thinking about it, I really believe in premonitions now. I think that there has to be some kind of connection. Some people will have a premonition, and then what they saw happens a month or a week after that, so it was freaky that this happened the day after my dream.

Carlos
Colombia

Chapter 45

A Poem From Beyond

Today is the four-year anniversary of my grandfather's death, so I thought it would be appropriate to share the story of what I believe was him communicating with me from beyond the grave.

This happened when I was about 16 years old. My grandfather was dying of cancer, and we knew it was going to happen pretty soon. At the time I was a very, very hardcore atheist. I was miserable because I didn't believe in anything, and I had no comfort whatsoever that he was going to be in a better place; I couldn't take the same kind of comfort in religion that my family seemed to be able to take. At the time, I was just kind of a depressed teenager; the only love of my life was my American Literature class in 11th grade. I loved this class, I loved my teacher...I loved everything about the class. It was one of the only classes I liked—I was close to flunking everything else. Anyhow, one of the poems—and this is going to be important, so bear with me—one of the poems we read was "Thanatopsis" by the American poet William Cullen Bryant. What made this poem so special was that it was one of the first and only poems written to comfort people about death, but with no mention of religion—no mention of heaven or spirituality or any of those popular Christian virtues.

This was a very controversial poem at the time, and it stated things like, "Don't be afraid of death, because you're going to where William Shakespeare and Julius Caesar are." Instead of "to where Jesus is," you know? Things like that. At the time I read the poem I thought, *That's nice, but I don't believe in anything either way. I don't believe in an afterlife either way, and wherever my grandfather is going he's just going to disappear and we're never going to see him again.* It was very difficult.

So, after he passed away, about a month later at Thanksgiving, my grandmother, his widow, was visiting my mother. My mother loves old, antique books, so my grandmother had brought over a bunch of old books that my grandfather had—and he had a lot of books. She just picked a random handful of books to bring and give to my mom. So my mom invited me to come into her room and take a look at the books. There were a couple of piles of them, and the jackets were missing, so there was no writing on the covers or on the spine, so I didn't know what they were.

I reached into one of the random piles, I pulled out a random book, I turned to a random page in the book, and there was the poem "Thanatopsis," the first page of it, by William Cullen Bryant. And, you know, to a skeptic this might be kind of anticlimactic, but to me at the time, when I didn't believe in anything, and the only way anyone could get me to express any interest in life or anything was through this literature class that I was obsessed with, you know, that was the only way that someone could have spoken to me. Of all the books that my grandmother could have brought, then out of all the books in that pile, then out of all the pages I could have turned to...you know? It was "Thanatopsis"! So, to this day, I strongly, strongly believe that this was my grandfather trying to contact me in the only way that he knew how to reach me, through this poem.

Everything's changed since then. It wasn't just that one event, although I think that event may have opened me up, made me think twice. But since then, as an adult now, I'm a very spiritual person, a very, very highly spiritual person. That was one of the first events to kind of trigger that trans-formation for me, so I'm very grateful to my grandfather for that.

Caity
New Mexico

Chapter 46

Goodbye Sunny

This was another one of those events that brought about my shift in spirituality, if you will, and this happened when I was 18, when I was leaving for college. My beloved Labrador Sunny was very sick. I had grown up with him; we had gotten him when I was 4. Now he was very sick, and we knew he had to be put down. I told my dad, "When I go to college, do what you've got to do, and don't tell me. I'll come home over Thanksgiving break and I'll know that the dog is gone, and that'll be that." I just couldn't handle the heartache.

So, I went to college. I didn't even make it to the first day of classes. The college was out of state, nine hours away, and I hated it and wanted to come home. I called my mom, and I was like, "Please come get me! I want to come home; I've got to get out of here." My mom and my stepdad came and picked me up, and I was so happy because I was thinking, "Oh, good! I can go home and see my dog again, and I get more time with him." When I called my dad to let him know I was coming home, he said, "You told me to just do what I have to do, so the day after you left I put Sunny to sleep."

My heart was just broken. I think above all, it was that I didn't get to say goodbye, really. I didn't get any closure, and that's why it was so hard to deal with.

That night, my mom and my stepdad and I were at a hotel, getting ready to head back home the next day. I fell asleep and had a dream that was very different from the way I normally dream. It was more lucid, more vivid, and it was just strangely real. In this dream, I'm back in my child-hood home, in the home where my dog Sunny grew up, and where I grew up. In the dream he is outside barking to come in. And I recognize his bark and I think, *Oh, gosh, how can this possibly be you? You're not supposed to be here any-more; you're supposed to be somewhere else.*

But anyway, I let him in. And he comes in and again I'm al-most scolding him, *Sunny, you're not supposed to be here any-more; you passed away, remember?* He looks at me, and with-out speaking or using any language it was sort of like...telepathic, but there were still no words used. It was just...I knew what he was trying to say. It was just a "Well, I thought you wanted to say goodbye and I wanted to say goodbye to you too, so let's just say goodbye and spend a couple more minutes together."

My heart just melted, so I sit down and he rolls over as usual, and I start rubbing his belly. And then, you know, I was thinking, *Okay, Sunny, it was really great to see you, but I feel like you really shouldn't be here. Something feels wrong about you being here.* Just as I'm thinking that, there is this incredibly loud crashing sound—my mom and my stepdad both heard it, too; we all woke up with a jolt. To this day we have no idea what it was. It was about 4 o'clock in the morning, and it woke all of us up. In that moment I heard this...almost like a faint suction sound. And I felt that there was something that had been right next to me, and it was lifted and gone. And so I definitely feel that was my dog coming back to say goodbye to me. And it's amazing, to this day I have no explanation for that.

Caity
New Mexico

Chapter 47

Nana at Night

When I heard your podcast, the one called "Called From the Grave," with the girl's grandfather, I had this really strong compulsion to talk about it, because I definitely identified with what she felt, so...

Alright, well, just to give you some background information, my family and I grew up in an all-wooden two-story house in an old town in Florida. The only way to get to the bottom floor was through a wooden spiral staircase. Growing up, no one went to the bottom floor of the house, because the atmosphere was just really thick and heavy, and as a kid I was terrified. I would never go down there. I even remember my sister sleeping upstairs on the couch. And when we entered the house, we would only enter directly onto the second floor. So, later, growing up, I learned that there had been a lot of abuse going on, and a lot of it in my sister's bedroom, so I don't know if that had something to do with not wanting to be down there. I've recently learned that if there's a lot of trauma going on with children, sometimes that can manifest things. But I don't know.

Anyway, during that time, my parents were going through a divorce, so I was spending a lot of time with my grandmother. And when I was a kid, I would feel like I was there for months, but it could have been weeks. I was very, very close with her.

I knew that she had been ill while on her vacation, and that my mom had gone to see her, and I slept upstairs. I fell asleep on this green, Victorian couch, and I had a dream. My grandmother came to me in my dream and she said "Sarah, come here, I have something for you."

And she led me to the top of the spiral staircase, and at that time I was really scared that she was going to ask me to go downstairs. As I got to the staircase, she leaned out and touched my hand. And when she touched my hand, it was like an electric shock, and I immediately woke up. When I woke up, I was sitting straight up on the couch, and I was really confused and really scared, and my father asked me what was going on. So I explained to him that I saw my Nana, and she told me that she had something for me, and she touched me, and then I had woken up. He soon informed me that she had passed away, and perhaps this was her way of saying goodbye to me. But I was really, really scared by it. To this day, my family has a running joke with me, which is, "Don't talk about Nana at night," because it scared me so badly. With the fear I also had a tremendous amount of guilt, because as much as it scared me, I didn't want her to think that I didn't love her, or that I didn't appreciate her coming to me. It was just something that I couldn't handle.

This followed me through college, and Nana would often appear in my dreams. She always had the same introduction: "Sarah, I'm going to come to you now, okay? Don't be scared." And there would be times when I'd be like, "Oh no, Nana, please don't come see me tonight, I'm really scared." And there would be other times I'd be like "Oh, okay," you know? Once I got past the initial vision of seeing her, it was okay, but it was just that anticipation of her coming, and me knowing what that experience was going to be, that I couldn't handle.

I didn't necessarily believe in a god, and I don't necessarily believe in one now, but praying was the only thing I could do to stop the experience. During my high school years I'd sit there in bed, asking, "God, please don't let me see anything tonight. Don't let anybody talk to me. I just want to go to bed." It was all I could really do to try to avoid those kinds of experiences. When she came to me, she didn't seem to have a significant message. She would just say, "I'm going to come see you now; don't be scared." So, I don't know. It's just my experience.

I haven't seen her in my dreams in a really long time. I will say that my husband has been fighting some of his own personal demons, and there was a time that it was getting really hard. I was cooking dinner in the kitchen and he was outside, and I smelled roses. It was what my grandmother always smelled like. I booked it out of the kitchen as fast as I could, and I pulled my husband in and asked, "Do you smell that?" He couldn't pinpoint it. So, for me, it wasn't really validated, but that was the first thing that I had possibly experienced from her in a really long time.

This kind of phenomenon is sort of like the deep ocean, to me. I know it exists; I know it's there. Here and there I'm interested to learn more about it, but I have a respect for it. It's an entire world on its own; I don't belong there, and I am okay with that. I'm okay with keeping my distance, and a part of me is really envious of people who can sleep in a dark room night after night, and not ever feel uncomfortable, you know?

I appreciate it that she chose to come to me, but the whole thing kind of confuses me. Like I said, I never felt that she had a significant message, and I don't know why, when she came to me in the first place, she said, "Sarah, come here, I have something for you." I don't know why she didn't just say, "I'm saying goodbye." All of it was kind of confusing.

Sarah
Florida

Chapter 48
Uncle Ted's Bed

This haunted bed has been in our family for a few generations. It was my Great Uncle Ted's when he was a child, and, unfortunately, he committed suicide, I think in the 1940s. It was at my great-grandmother's house until she was too old to really take care of the house, and then it was passed down to my parents and became kind of like a guest bed. About five years ago when I was visiting them, they assigned me to sleep in it.

I hadn't heard that it was his, or the history behind it; it was just always there in the house. It's an old wooden bed.

So I went to bed as usual, and that night I had this really wild dream that I was driving on the highway in Buffalo, where we lived, on the skyway—a highway bridge that follows the beachfront of Lake Erie. I was looking out the window of the passenger side in the dream, and my mother was driving. It was really windy up there. I was looking out the window, and I kept seeing ghost faces touching their faces against the window and tapping on the window. I was really freaked out by this dream, and I remember waking up and the bed was shaking as if it was your car on this kind of bridge highway, shaking because it's so high up in the wind. There was tapping as if the ghost faces were tapping on the passenger side window. I had woken up, but the bed was still shaking and there was still tapping, you know? And I was terrified.

I kept very still in the bed, thinking maybe I had turned in my sleep and that's why the bed was moving and there was tapping, but it continued. The tapping went on for about 30 seconds to about a minute, and I was just trying to muster up enough courage to say "STOP!" I said, "Please stop!" Then it did—instantly.

Meg
Arizona

Chapter 49

Breaking News, in My Dreams

I guess you could call me somewhat of a skeptic; I'm kind of the "I have to see it to believe it" type. I'll listen to paranormal stories and I'll have my doubts. But premonitions in particular have come to me within dreams, and it's been interesting, to say the least. The first one was about an international news event. But I didn't know that until the next morning when I heard about it on CNN or Fox News, or whatever news station I was listening to that day.

First of all, I should probably explain that I'm originally from Santiago, Chile. I was adopted by an American family, and my dream was about my home country. In it, I was standing on a hillside with...I guess I can identify them as native Chileans. We were staring at this volcano that was slowly erupting, and it covered the countryside. We were all running from it as it was erupting; it was spewing ash and creating a giant gray cloud. I found it weird that I kind of experienced it through a first-person point of view, not like an "I'm floating above my body" kind of dream. The next morning, I woke up to find out that indeed a volcano had erupted in Santiago overnight. So it was the night of the eruption that I had the dream, and I had no way of knowing this—I was in Florida. It was a little...exciting, and scary at the same time.

I wish I could have done something. Would anyone have believed me? If only the dream had happened a couple of days earlier. I do share my dreams with my girlfriend and all of my family, just in case anything like that could happen again. I wish I could have told somebody beforehand, because it coming true was just wild.

And that's not the only premonition I've had. The next one was in a dream as well, and it was also an international event. I don't know if you recall, but a while back there was an Airbus A330 plane that went down. It was an Air France airliner. Everyone had heard about that, but that's not what I experienced in my dream. About a month after the Air France incident, I dreamt that we had another Airbus go down, and that there was one survivor, a child. I viewed the plane kind of going erratically, flying erratically in circles around me, and I was next to the coast in the dream. I was watching a plane just fly erratically in circles, and then finally going down, crashing into the ocean.

I didn't think much of it, because I try to connect dreams to what's going on in my life, so I kind of thought about it like, *Maybe I don't have control over a situation for the time being*, like at work or in my personal life. In the morning, I listened to the *Today Show* on my iPhone and I heard breaking news about an Airbus going down in the Indian Ocean, with one survivor, and I was just in shock. I couldn't believe it, for a dream like that to come true a second time.

Daniel
Florida

Chapter 50

Dream Invasion

It happened I guess about eight years ago, a few years before I married my wife. We were staying in this old house that always had some weird things associated with it—doors closing; just odd situations. We had roommates and we were all frightened of something in the house. We talked about it, but we were never sure what it was.

One night we were all sleeping and I was having a dream that my wife and I were in bed when this figure, this dark shadowy figure started choking her, and I was staring at her, trying to get this figure off her but I was paralyzed. I couldn't move.

We'd come to find out we were both having the dream simultaneously. I didn't know this at the time. I shot awake and started freaking out, and she shot awake at the exact same time freaking out as well. I asked her, "What is wrong with you?" and she told me the exact same story from my dream, except in hers she was being held down by something. She was looking at me while she was being held down and I had this terrified look on my face.

In this dream, we were almost like two actors, and my point of view was from kind of the hero who was going to save her, and her point of view was the person being attacked. It was crazy. I never experienced anything like that since and I don't expect I ever will.

Chris
Arkansas

Part IV: Something out of This World

Some stories defy categorization, and these can be some of the most suspenseful and engaging tales on the CAMPFIRE program. Questions of synchronicity, of seeing something in the future and changing it, of telekinesis, or of experiencing poltergeist activity around a particular relative...are these phenomena supernatural in nature? Are they caused by our own emotions, or by fate? Who knows?

One thing is for sure: These stories bring a chill that makes me long for another log to throw on the fire!

Chapter 51

The Case of the Bookcase

I have very strong intuition, and as I get older, I think I have to listen to that more and more, because it's come through several times. I think the strongest, most significant incident in my lifetime, as far as intuition goes, is what happened when I was visiting Budapest many years ago. This was about '79 or '81, before my husband and I had our children.

He and I went to Europe for a bit of a holiday, before we had our family, when we were footloose and fancy-free. I have relatives and family there, and I'd visited quite a lot when I was growing up. I wanted my husband to get to know Hungary too, so we were going to stay in Budapest. My father had come to Budapest a few weeks before we were due to arrive, and he rented a small apartment for us so that we would have a place to stay and not have to worry about that when we arrived. It was an apartment that would be shared with a man who lived there. He had a huge apartment, and had a room there that he rented out to people.

So we arrived very late at night at the airport, and we were extremely tired, because it was a long journey. My cousin picked us up and drove us to this apartment. The fellow showed us the room, and it was this huge old-fashioned apartment, a great big room, and he said, "Okay, it's really late at night; don't worry about unpacking all your things. We'll leave and you can settle in." My cousin said, "Yeah, we're going to leave, too, and we'll come by and visit in the morning."

I still don't really understand the feelings that I started getting at that point, but they were so strong, it was almost not in my control. What I had noticed was that the beds were separated (in Europe they often are in apartments—they would have one bed in one corner and another bed in another corner, or the two beds would be separated with a little night table). My husband and I had been married maybe one or two years; we weren't newlyweds, but I looked at the beds and I said to my husband, my cousin, her husband, and the fellow who was renting the apartment: "Those beds have to be moved." And they kind of looked at me incredulously. It was 2:30 or 3 o'clock in the morning, and their expressions were like, *Wait a minute. We're not going to start moving furniture now.* We're talking about heavy, European-style furniture and exhausted travelers. They looked at me and said, "Well, you can wait 'til morning. Why do you have to do this now?" And I stood so firmly on the ground there it was like I was nailed to the floor, and I wouldn't budge. And I said, "No, you have to move the beds." For the life on him, my husband couldn't understand why I was being so adamant.

It was just like something outside myself was controlling me, and I just insisted and insisted. Finally, very reluctantly, the men picked up these beds and I directed them. I said, "They have to be on that other wall, way over on the other side." So they moved them, and we flopped into bed as soon as that was done. That was it.

All of a sudden—I don't know what time it was, but it was still dark—there was this huge crash. It was totally dark; there was no light around at all, because this particular apartment faced into a hillside. My first thought was that a car had come over the hill and gone off the road and come in through the window, because there was the sound of splintering glass and just a tremendous crash. My husband said, "Don't get out of bed." He gingerly stepped out, trying to avoid maybe stepping on some glass, and found a light switch way on the other side by the door. What had happened was that the huge, heavy bookcase with beveled glass doors and thick encyclopedias or other books in it that was attached to the wall had crashed down onto the floor. One of the beds had been underneath that bookcase before it was moved. Whoever had been sleeping in that bed when the bookcase had come down...well, they would have been...instantly gone. Dead, right there on the spot.

The thing is, I didn't really perceive the bookcase to begin with, and when I noticed the bed, I wasn't noticing the bookcase there. I didn't think along those lines...I just knew that the beds had to be together; we had to sleep together, not separate, and that the beds had to be on the other wall.

Not moving the other bed to where the bookcase was, but the other wall. And it was just beyond my control.

The fellow that was in the apartment, his rooms were way down a hallway. In the morning, we approached and knocked on his door and said, "Look, come see what happened during the night." He was just astounded, because he grew up in that apartment; it was his childhood home. He said that that bookcase was his grandfather's bookcase, and it had been on the wall when he was a boy, and he slept under that bookcase, and he would have never imagined that it could have come off the wall. After all those years, just that very night. And he didn't hear anything. So, you know, after that experience, I always, always say to myself (although I don't always follow through with it), I tell myself to listen to what I'm feeling because it's very strong.

Judith
Canada

Chapter 52

An Unexpected Visitor

I'm sure a lot of your listeners are horror movie fans—or at least some of them. So, the easiest way to explain the place where I grew up is...well, it's like the location of the house from *Evil Dead*. Picture a cabin in the woods, with a dirt road leading to it, lots of trees. Unlike in *Evil Dead*, though, it was a fairly nice house, although it was definitely out there in the middle of nowhere. It was a little spooky. No neighbors, no noise whatsoever at night. Maybe a howling wolf or something. It was in northern Georgia, the Appalachian foot hills. There is a bit of history with the area surrounding my house: I'd heard it was a historical battleground during the Civil War. As a child, I often roamed out in the woods, exploring, and I'd found several burial mounds, as well as remnants of older houses—things like that. Civil War bullets and things.

When I was 18, I was home by myself one night when I heard a knocking coming from the walls. Now, this didn't scare me at the time, because my friends, who knew I could be frightened by living out there by myself, primarily, had shown up on several occasions and knocked on the walls before—a little prank. Good clean fun. They'd even sometimes wake me up on the weekends when I was sleeping, because it was something to do—and there is not a lot to do in North Georgia when you're 18.

So, figuring it was them again, I went outside, and I said, "Oh, that's really funny you guys," and I walked around the perimeter of the house once, and there was nothing going on. No one there. So, I just guessed a bird flew into the wall or something. I didn't know. I went back inside and continued to watch *Battlebots* on TV.

About three or four minutes later, I started hearing the same knocking coming from the roof. And I thought it was just wind...trees. So, I went outside again and looked. There was no wind whatsoever; it was completely still that night. I walked back inside, but was starting to get a little concerned.

Just a few minutes later, the knocking started coming from the ground. Now, we don't have a basement or anything, so I couldn't check that. It didn't make sense, how the noise could even generate from the ground, and about this time I noticed that my cat was sitting right beside me. It was almost never that affectionate, and it was pushing itself up against me, staring at the source of this noise, and it freaked out.

The funny thing was that I was grabbing the cat, screaming, "You protect me!"

And that wasn't even the end yet. After that, I thought maybe someone or a group of people were playing a very big prank on me. So, I went and got a very large knife and sat in the middle of the room and waited for this to stop. The cat was sitting there with me, and suddenly the knocking started coming from the walls *and* the ceiling *and* the floor, and it just kept going while increasing in intensity.

I sat there thinking, *I don't have any other options. I'm at home; there's nowhere to run. I'm just going to sit here and wait this out.* It just kept getting creepier. After 10 minutes, it still did not stop. Finally, I left and went to stay with a friend for the night.

I thought maybe it was some kind of residual haunting from the war. I don't know if it was the house itself, because I only had one other experience there. I thought maybe it was something passing through.

Six or seven years prior to the knocking story, when I was 11 or so, I was walking through the kitchen at night-time when my parents were already asleep. I turned to look down a hallway and there was just a glowing ball of light, about the size of a Yorkshire terrier. Now, I say that because we had a Yorkshire terrier, and immediately I thought, *Oh, it's Muffy.* But it couldn't have been Muffy because it was white and glowing! And as soon as I looked at it, it took off down the hallway, and it slammed into a couple of walls, and it disappeared into one of them. It all happened so fast that I thought maybe I just imagined it or something, but it was a little too elaborate for a figment of my imagination.

As I said, I don't know that if the house is haunted per se; the things I experienced might just have been something moving through. I don't know how the mechanics of that work. If I thought something was going to happen again,

I'd definitely like to go back. That's an option; the house is still in the family. But I just don't think anything would happen again. In 18 years of living there, I had only two strange experiences. I've gone out on my own, trying to do some ghost hunting, because this is obviously an interest of mine, and I've never come across anything in all of my searching like this. It scared me at the time, but I'd be really interested to find out what it was.

Zach
Florida

Chapter 53

Mr. Synchronicity

I've had moments, I think as most people have, when I've had feelings of premonition or something, when you can predict the next song that comes on the radio, or you get a flash of something about to happen, and then it does.

Those kinds of things. Hard to define; hard to write down or document.

A few unusual incidents occurred that lead up to my main story.

Maybe 12 years ago I had a dream one night about a specific government agency. Not anything black-ops or anything like that, just a state agency, and I woke up the next day thinking, *That was a strange dream. Why would I dream about that?* That night, I got together with a friend of mine and a new girl he was dating, and I asked her, "What do you do?" She worked for that same state agency that I had dreamt about. Very strange.

Moments like that have happened throughout my life. Last year, I found myself reconnecting with a lot of friends from the past, and there was one former coworker I particularly wanted to seek out. I made myself a note to see if I could find him online or contact some friends and see what was going on with this guy. I forgot to do it, but the next day I got a friend request from another coworker on Facebook, and the person I was looking to find was a friend with this other coworker. So, strange coincidence there. That got me thinking, *What else? I wonder if I could affect this outcome somehow.* So I asked myself to think of someone I hadn't connected with in a long time. I thought, *My old college roommate!* So, a few days later I spent probably 30 minutes to an hour online trying to find this old friend of mine, and had no luck at all. I couldn't find him; couldn't find a phone number; nothing whatsoever. So I gave up. The very next day, he signed up for Facebook and I was the first person he sought out. Fifteen years after I last spoke with him, he seeks me out the day after I was looking for him. Uncanny!

Those stories lead up to the main story of synchronicity I wanted to tell you about. I know I'm a Cancer, but I'm fairly skeptical about astrology. It doesn't seem logical to me. I've read lots of things about it, and I understand it, but it still doesn't fit into my worldview.

Still, I've found throughout the course of my life that I've had strong connections with other Cancers, by coincidence, and those born under Leo as well. My wife is a Leo, my oldest daughter is a Leo, and I have another daughter who is a Cancer, actually born on my birthday. So, that's a happy coincidence. *(Author's Note: Jim Harold is also a Cancer.)*

About 11 years ago, I was on vacation with some friends, and we were out on the town. We started talking with another group of people, and something about one of the women in this group immediately seemed familiar to me. I felt that I knew her somehow. But I'd never met her before. So we started talking to this group of people and I started talking to this woman.

It turns out we had a lot in common. We immediately had a connection, and she also had the same birthday as I do. Afterward, we kept in contact for about a year and a half, I guess. I never saw her again; we just kept in contact through mail and e-mail. But after about a year and a half, our acquaintance just tapered off.

About eight and a half years later, a week after my wife and I separated, I was updating my day planner and I saw this woman's birthday. I always carry it over, even though it's the same as mine and I always remember it. That very day she reached out and found me again! I received a message from her, after it had been so long since I had last talked with her. She found me the very day that I was writing her birthday down in my day planner.

One of the things that we had talked about during our original correspondence was our mutual enjoyment of a well-known writer named Jim Harrison who was from her home town in Michigan. Later that day, that she contacted me, as I was driving home, I was listening to a literary podcast in my car, and they read a poem of the day. Guess what. The poem that day was by this writer we both love—Jim Harrison! I found that a sort of amazing coincidence as well.

Now that I was back in contact with her again, the coincidences became too many to list. One after another—things like similarities in our family names, or experiences that had happened to us over time, or "I was listening to this particular song today," "I was listening to that exact same song today"; little things like that. After a couple of months, we found somehow that this connection between the two of us was becoming a bit distracting. She was married and felt that this was not the right time for this to happen—whatever this inexplicable connection was—so we just stopped talking and went on with our lives.

I sent her a package for her birthday with a box of chocolates or something like that in it. I didn't know it when I sent it, but inside the box there was another poem. That day when I was driving home I listened to the literary podcast again. The poem that day was the same one that was in the box that I had sent her! Amazing.

I went on vacation last year and on the flight home, another weird bit of synchronicity happened. I was reading a book, something along the lines of ''How to Write a Novel in a Month." I started talking to this woman next to me, and she asked if I would I ever want to write a novel. I said I thought it would be fascinating. She asked what I would write about. I mentioned that I thought it would be fascinating to explore synchronicity: unexplained coincidences between people, and connections.

She asked for an example, so I told her this story plus some of the other coincidences that have happened in my life. She thought they were interesting. For an hour-and-a-half flight, I talked to her nonstop. Again, it was this connection with somebody, kind of a like-mindedness, and the conversation just kind of flows easily, right?

At the end of the flight, we both got up to leave, and she said she thought the coincidences around my birthday were particularly interesting. I said yes, that even my daughter shares my birthday. She asked when my birthday was and I told her. She said she knew I was going to say that! She pulled out her driver's license and showed me, and there in black and white it was absolutely the same day as mine. Amazing!

Steven
California

Chapter 54

Staying for the Credits

It was the first or second week of April in 2004, and my wife and I decided to go see a movie. *Hellboy* had just come out so we went to the local movie theater here in the northwest part of New Jersey. It was just a typical day, and I'm not sure if it was a Saturday or a Sunday, but we drove to the movie theater, pulled up, purchased tickets for, I believe it was the 2:45 show—the afternoon matinee.

We just purchased tickets, went in and did the typical stuff—went to the concession counter and purchased popcorn and a soda—then proceeded into one of the movie theaters. This is one of those Cineplexes that have multiple screens—seven or 10, something like that.

We went over to the boy who was taking tickets and he ripped them in half and pointed us in the right direction. We proceeded to go over toward our theater and went inside. I like to get to the theater a little earlier, because I don't like to fumble around when it's dark and they're playing the previews. So we entered at 2:30, 2:35, something like that. When we got there, and pushed through the doors and went in, the lights were already down and there was something on the screen playing, and I was like, "Oh, darn it."

So, we had to fumble around to find a seat, kind of in the middle-center, and we thought previews were playing. After sitting down for a minute or so, my wife and I kind of looked at each other, and were like, "These aren't previews." It was actually the ending of the movie we had gone to see. We could see that *Hellboy* was on the screen, there was a lot of stuff going on, and after three or four minutes of that going on the movie ended.

We realized it was the actual movie playing, and we were kind of wondering what the heck was going on here. So, the lights came up, and the people were doing what they do when they get up, starting to stretch and head out the back of the theater.

We both got up too. I got up first and I stopped somebody on the way out and said, you know, "I'm just curious, what show is this?" The gentleman had said this was the 2:45 show. So, that was the show we were going to see. I didn't really think much of it; I went back over and said to my wife, "This gentleman says that this is the 2:45 show," which was the show that we were to go see. We got up and followed when everybody exited and went out the back door.

I went out to the lobby, and I saw the kid who took my ticket, which was literally minutes ago. I asked, "You remember me?" and he said yes. (I was a cancer patient at the time, so I didn't have hair, and I guess he kind of remembered me from that.) So he said, "Sure, I remember you," and I said, "We had tickets to go see the 2:45 show," and he said "Yeah, that just let out."

At that time, I wasn't shocked, but then I looked down at my watch. I should point out I'm kind of a time person. I collect watches and I'm a stickler for time. I looked down at my watch, and it was around 4:47. So when we entered the theater, it was 2:35, 2:30, something like that, and then it was 4:47.

So I looked at my wife, and she checked her watch, and we kind of realized that something wasn't right. How could it be 4:47, when we just walked into the movie theater?

We kind of just looked at each other, still not getting crazy with this, and we went back into the movie theater and spoke about it. Then we went back outside to the lobby, checked the clocks there, and then looked outside. It was early April and you could tell that it was later in the day than when we had gotten there. The sun had gone lower...and I think we just realized then that something weird had happened. How does something like this happen? We were just dumbfounded. I didn't know what to think or what to say.

People have said to me, "Oh, that's missing time." Still, it doesn't seem that way, because we walked through that door into that movie theater and instantaneously it was two hours later, just like in the blink of an eye.

Because we were confused, we thought that maybe we'd gone into the wrong showing—there's seven or 10 screens there—so we walked around, and I asked the young guy, "Is this playing on other screens?" He said, "No, this is the only one it's playing on." I had told him what had happened, and he said, "You came in a couple of hours ago," and that's when I felt like someone had punched me in the gut, and I was like, "Oh, my God."

My wife is a straight-shooter; she's not into anything that's paranormal or bizarre so I'm glad she was there with me, because it validates the fact that something really bizarre happened. Then, we walked around the theater for a while, in such disbelief that something like that could happen, and then we actually went in and watched...I think it was the 5 o'clock show.

You know, I still had the soda in my hand. We still had the popcorn—I've had people ask me if the popcorn was gone, you know? And "Did you feel anything?" And I've said no. We felt normal; everything was normal, but it was weird. The sun was down farther, they day had gone on... how do you tell this story to people? Nobody believes you, or they think you're crazy.

I have no idea what happened. You know, I was going through a really hard time then. I had cancer, and it had spread all through my body. So we were going to the movies a lot, just for a distraction, you know, just for me to be around people, that sort of thing. But you know, in my mind, I was in such good spirits, I was in such a positive state. I have no idea. I don't know what happened. The only time we ever talk about it is when that movie comes on, and we'll be like, "That's the movie when the time thing happened," and people will ask, "What do you mean, 'the time thing'?" and we'll tell them, and they're like, "That's crazy," you know? People don't believe it...

Marko
New Jersey

Chapter 55

A Commotion From Above

This happened when I was living in New Orleans in a duplex. I guess it had been a private home and at some time they made it into four apartments. I eventually ended up living in three of the four apartments, because the rent was very reasonable and it was very comfortable. The weird goings-on there never really bothered me that much; I just thought it was very interesting.

About the most bizarre thing that ever happened there was one night when I was getting ready to go to bed. I was with my boyfriend at the time. We were just about to go to sleep, and all of a sudden we heard all kinds of racket from upstairs, and it was strange because it was a Sunday night and we knew the people upstairs, and there was a lot of noise. Yet, there wasn't any talking or screaming. It sounded like some kind of altercation, like things were being dragged across the floor and thrown. There was a baby crying during the whole experience.

I knew the guy upstairs had a girlfriend who had a child, but it was not a baby. The child was 3 or 4 years old. And nothing loud ever happened up there, really. So, I thought at the time it was very strange. It just kept going on. Then, finally, we heard what sounded like something hitting the floor with a huge bang, and something obviously being dragged across the floor. After that, then we heard something going down steps. Wooden steps. That was weird because the interior steps had been walled in years before, and there were exterior steps but they were metal.

The sound of something falling down metal steps and wooden steps is very different. About an hour into this commotion, we just looked at each other, and I said, "I'm just going to sleep now. Something obviously weird is going on." All this time, the baby is crying and crying. As soon as I said that, the baby—I still get chills thinking about it now—the sound of the baby just stopped from above our heads. All of a sudden it sounded like it was coming from across the street.

It was just so bizarre. I feel that apartment building, the duplex, had been around for a long time, and that there was something there. Now, I've lived in New Orleans and in Savannah, and those are two of the top haunted places supposedly in the United States, but I've also lived in other places where I've never—well, I've never felt that kind of activity here in Houston, so...

When I saw my upstairs neighbor later in the week, I asked him about the commotion. His name was Tommy, and I said, "Tommy, I don't know what was going on Sunday night. Y'all were really kind of going at it, and it was very awkward for us." He looked at me like I was just insane. He said, "What are you talking about, Susan? We were in Baton Rouge on Sunday night!"

Susan
Texas

Chapter 56

Things Happen Here

I've been married to my wife for about 16 years, and I can't believe some of stuff that's actually happened to her—to us. I'm a former United States Marine, and I've never encountered anyone with psychic ability before. I've never understood some of the stuff that I've seen, but some of what has happened in this apartment I'm in is just extraordinary.

My wife has seen arms coming out of the dishwasher. It sounds crazy...an arm coming out of a dishwasher doesn't make any sense at all. She told me that these arms were coming out, and she thought there was a kid inside. She looked inside and there wasn't anything there.

One time we were just going through a set of photographs that we had (we have hundreds that we've taken from different times in this apartment), and we came across something stunning. We have a corner space that's totally unusual. The kids won't go near it. They say they feel a presence there, and I never understood that until we saw the photograph we ran across that day. It shows a...it appears to be a naked woman from the knees up. You can't see anything beyond the shoulders, but it looks totally clear. There's nothing that could be in that corner, because there's a chair and a little table, so there's nothing else that could physically be there. The photo shows everything else, but it also shows something there. It's totally clear. You can even see the veins in this thing's legs. We don't understand what it is. I think I'm the one who took it, because I remember taking photographs at that time, but I don't remember there being anything in the picture at that time. So when I looked at it, with the series of photographs that we got coming back, I just couldn't understand it. So, I asked everyone that was present, "What the hell is this?" Nobody understood it. And actually, the person that we did take a photograph of at that time just kind of freaked out because this thing's in the upper right-hand corner. One of the people who was in the photograph won't come into this apartment at all.

Back to my wife. On three different occasions, I've actually heard voices calling her name, and there's nobody there. Absolutely no one. I know that sounds crazy, but there's nobody there. I've heard it clear as day, and do not understand it. I've looked everywhere. This is a small apartment.

There are other things going on here I cannot explain. There was a hand floating around that the kids saw, and that scared them to death. They won't come into this apartment anymore. I've actually considered moving, but I love the place we're living; it's right on the public transportation line. We can go back and forth; I don't even have to use my car anymore. It's picturesque, there's trees and everything...I don't want to move. I've been here so long that the price is perfect, and I don't have to worry about it. But, there are these strange things that keep happening.

I'll tell you what, it doesn't bother me because I've been here so long that I'm kind of used to this stuff. I see stuff out of the corner of my eye, like smoke, and neither of us smoke! Yet, we see puffs of smoke around the apartment. I don't understand that at all. I go look to make sure there's nothing on fire! My wife likes candles. She likes lighting candles. She says prayers. She's Catholic; she does the candle thing. But every time I've looked and found smoke, I don't see anything burning. So there's another thing that I don't understand that at all.

When we moved here, for some reason, a whirlwind of things started to happen. My wife saw creatures on a building next to us. Apparently the person next door, downstairs, before the manager moved in, actually witnessed the same event. She claims she was sitting outside and she heard dogs barking really crazily, and she saw something out of the corner of her eye, in the pitch-black: Three little people—she described them as people—jumped up onto a building next door, onto the roof. She could see their silhouettes by the light on the street next to us. And apparently she sat there, and she made a movement to get up, to kind of get a better look at them, and they all looked at her at the same time, and it kind of freaked her out because they all looked at the same time, kind of like in unison, and they were all the same size, and according to her they jumped from house to house to house, very quickly. There's something like 15 feet between each of these houses. I'm looking at it right now. Fifteen feet between house to house, and they did it in three or four seconds.

The neighborhood dogs were just going crazy, and kept going crazy for four or five hours. My wife told me when I came home that I was not going to believe what happened. She explained it to me, and I thought, *God, what the hell could that be?* I looked out there, and saw the big space between the houses. I don't think anything other than a marathon runner could actually run and jump to make a 15-foot span from house to house, all the way down the block. That doesn't make any sense.

I actually considered putting salt around the place, because I looked on the Internet, and in a couple of places, the advice was to take salt and make a circle around everything, but I never did that. It doesn't bother me here, it's just that things happen.

Daniel
United States

Chapter 57

The Spirits Woke Me Up

The whole thing was pretty odd. I woke up at 6 o'clock in the morning after I'd just gone to bed at probably 3 o'clock in the morning, so I only had about three hours of sleep. I couldn't seem to get back to sleep. I was wide awake and I wanted to go back to sleep. It took about four hours for me to finally doze off a little bit, and then something woke me up. It was really loud, and I wasn't sure what it was, but it scared me enough to wake me up.

I got up for a little bit and looked around. Nobody was home, so I didn't know what made the noise. I went back to bed. Again, I was trying to go to sleep and just as I was about to doze off, I heard it yet again, and then I realized that the noise sounded like I was in a dining hall. I was listening to people having conversations around me. I couldn't understand them at the time, but it was a kind of slow murmuring that you hear if you're in a restaurant, and it kind of got quieter and quieter, and then it finally faded away.

After it faded off, I thought, *Okay, that was a little odd, but I'm going to try to go back to sleep.* I'd experienced stuff like that before. I didn't think it was too odd, and I figured it was just going to go away. When I tried to go back to sleep I heard it again, only this time it got louder and there were more details to it. I heard a man telling a woman a joke, and I heard her laughing, and this time it kept getting louder instead of quieter.

So I sat up, and I was looking around, trying to figure out if there was something there, maybe, but I didn't see anything. So, I lay back down again and thought, *This time I'm really going to sleep*, so I closed my eyes and I was just about ready to get to sleep, and I heard it again, and it kept getting louder and louder. I heard the woman laughing and I heard the man telling the joke, but this time it was kind of on repeat, because I heard him telling the same joke (although I don't remember what it was now; the details have kind of slipped my mind since then). I heard him telling the joke, and I heard her laughing, and every time I'd hear her laughing, I'd see her in like a red dress or something, in my head. I couldn't see her face, but I could hear her.

I knew it wasn't a dream because after I started hearing it I would open my eyes and look at myself in the mirror across the room. That way I would know that I was awake. I know I was perfectly conscious of what was happening, because I was having perfectly conscious thoughts, like, *Okay, is this...what am I hearing?*

I kept trying to ignore it, and every time I would think, *Okay, this isn't real, this is a hallucination or something.* I was just covering my ears and trying to ignore it. But it kept getting louder and louder and louder and louder, until I finally said, "Okay, just shut up. I'm trying to sleep." And then it exploded. It felt like an explosion to me. And this is where it starts getting really odd. It felt like I was in an explosion because I heard the ringing in my ears, I went completely blind, and it felt like I couldn't move and my entire body went numb; I wasn't sure if I was able to move. I was trying to roll around, to see if I could move, but I wasn't sure if I was moving. So finally it faded away after about a minute or so—it felt a lot longer than that, but it did finally fade away after a minute—and I realized I had been lying on my side while this was happening, but when I came out of this state, I was lying on my back, so I did actually move. That's kind of what makes me think it wasn't sleep paralysis, because, first of all, I wasn't asleep, and second of all, if it was paralysis, I wouldn't have been able to move to my back.

Well, I went to check my phone. I couldn't grab my phone at first because my hand would go around it but I couldn't grab onto it. And so I finally grabbed my phone, and when I checked the time, the time was exactly 11:11.

A couple people have told me that maybe it was a spirit trying to get a hold of me, or trying to get my attention through the whole 11:11 thing. Somebody also told me that it was probably a partial out-of-body experience, too, because I wasn't fully unconscious, so it could have been that. Some people might think I'm insane, but I feel what I heard and saw was real.

Tiffany
Ohio

Chapter 58

Oh, Rats!

I grew up with a stepmom, and bizarre things always happened to her, particularly in one house we lived in with her. One of the first things I remember was when we were sitting down at dinner, and she suddenly grabbed her arm. She was in pain, she said. My dad asked, "What's the matter?" She said that something slapped her! She moved her hand, and you could actually see welts coming up on her arm. At first I thought that maybe she had done it herself, but the prints were opposite. You know when you grab your arm, your fingerprints are on the outside of your arm? Well these were on the inside of her arm.

Yeah, it was a little strange for us. We just kind of sat there and looked at her and thought, *Okay, then!* The craziest thing was, not too long after that, whenever she would sit down to watch television or something, it just seemed like rats would fall on her out of the blue.

It didn't matter where she sat, they always landed on her. And we were looking at the ceiling and everything, to make sure that they weren't crawling across the ceiling. We didn't know if they could do that or not, but.... Rats are pretty athletic, and can go almost anywhere. In this case, though, rats would appear from nowhere, and you'd never see a rat again. You wouldn't find an infestation or anything. They would just drop out of the sky and hit her! My dad set mouse traps out and everything, and got nothing. They would never get caught.

I should say that there were rats and there were mice. It was just...it was random. I'd heard of it raining cats and dogs, but...not mice and rats!

We had a "Cypress Knee" sitting on our TV. It's the stump of a tree that grows in the swamps in the southeast. They're not light, those things. They can be kind of heavy. My Dad had one that sat on top of the television. One time my stepmom was standing at the back door, talking to my dad, who was outside. I was standing in the doorway of my room, and I saw this Cypress Knee come floating from the living room into the kitchen. It was levitating, and it moved toward my stepmom. My dad was outside and through the window saw something behind her, and he said, "What's that?" She turned around, and as soon as she did, it dropped to the floor and rolled to her feet. Of course, I was standing in the doorway watching this as it happened. She looked at me, and I turned around and went back into my room. For a little while she was scared of me, because she thought I was the one making that stuff happen.

These particular things were directed at my stepmom, but there were other, more general things happening. At night we could hear things walking around by the bed. Just a constant pacing, back and forth. Soon after we moved out of this house, it burned down. It seemed that there was something strange in every house that we lived in, so long as my dad was married to her. The only thing that I can think of is that she said she used to do witchcraft, before she met my dad. She used to play with Ouija boards. Maybe that was drawing in those spirits.

We moved into this house, what they call a parsonage, which was a preacher's house, next to this church that was on the property. For some reason, the preacher just did not want to live in that house, so he lived somewhere else. Because it was available my dad decided that we'd move into it. Weird little things would happen there. You'd turn off the light in the bathroom (it had those old switches that you had to push down or up really hard to get the light to come on), and you'd take two steps out of the bathroom and it would turn back on. The switch would be up. It wasn't just an electrical problem; the actual physical switch would be in the opposite position from where you'd left it.

Also, the water faucets would turn on and off by themselves. We'd hear water running and go check the bathroom, and there was the water running. Of course, my dad was getting after us saying that we needed to turn off the water after we used it. We'd say, "But it was a ghost!" and of course he was like, "Yeah, right."

Stuff like that happened all the time in that house. But the big event that happened was around Christmastime. We had just come home from my grandmother's house and were standing on the porch, waiting to go into the house. My dad moved to put the key in the lock when the curtain that's on the front door pulled back. It pulled back but there was nobody standing there.

My stepmom was very pregnant with my brother at the time. I've never seen the woman move so fast in my life. She had cleared the steps and was out in the yard. I was up on the porch, and I backed up—there was a rail, thankfully, or I would have fallen in the bushes. My dad finished opening the door and then he went in to go turn on the light. Not every room in the house had a light switch; some rooms you had to go in and actually pull the string down from the ceiling light to turn the light on, and in the living room that was the case. So he went in to turn the light on, and then he came running out. He said something had slapped his hand when he turned the light on. I was holding our cat, and he grabbed it—this was a nightly ritual and my cat was used to it—and he tossed the cat in the house. My cat was usually fine with it, but this particular night my cat was not fine with it. My dad threw the cat in there, and the cat let out a yowl and ran out, down the street, and up the tallest tree he could find. And that cat didn't come down for three days. He stayed up in that tree.

My dad thought maybe there was somebody in the house, so he decided to go back in. He turned on the light, and as he did, he could hear running. The way the house was set up, you'd have to go through one bedroom to get to another bedroom, and then into the kitchen, and then on the other side you had the living room, then dining room, and that went into the kitchen as well. He thought that the running went to the bedrooms, so my dad went through the dining room into the kitchen. He reached the kitchen about the same time as the running noises, but there was nobody there. Our back door was locked—the screen door on it was locked, but the back door actually going out onto the porch was pushed the opposite way of how it was supposed to go. You pull it in to open it, but it was pushed out. So he managed to get through the door, and the screen door was still locked, and he could hear running across the grass, and he said that he was looking out the screen, and whatever was out there turned around, and it had glowing red eyes.

About a week later, after the porch incident, it was right after Christmas. My dad was sleeping and he said that he felt something shake him. So he woke up, and he said that there was something standing next to the bed, and all it did was point to the wall where—in his bedroom, the fireplace was up against the wall in the living room, and through his dresser he could see that there was a red glowing ball, and that's when he realized that the house was on fire, and he got everybody out of the house. He thinks that if whoever/whatever hadn't woken him up, we would have been in trouble.

We had a lot of stuff happen to us, and I think it was centered around my stepmom. I do because when I left the home, I didn't have that kind of stuff happening anymore. When my dad finally divorced her some years later, things calmed down for him as well. From the time that he married her, there was stuff that was happening all over the place.

Jacqui
Nevada

Chapter 59

Mind Over Matter

I was on YouTube looking up some video because I was bored, and I saw something they call a psi-wheel, that involved meditating a little bit. I decided to try it out. I've always believed mind over matter was possible; I'm a firm believer in that of that area of the paranormal. The psi-wheel wasn't too hard to make, really; I just took a needle and a bottle cap and a piece of paper and I set it up. I started looking at it to make it move, and it didn't really work out too well.

So I just kind of relaxed my mind a little bit, and, lo and behold, it started spinning. I sat up straight and I kind of freaked out. I'd never done anything like that before. And, you know, it was my first time even trying it, and I wasn't expecting to get that far at all.

I decided to take a little break after doing that, and I went out to the bathroom to get a drink of water and make sure I was fully awake. It was a little late: 9:30 or 10 o'clock. I went back to my room and stood about 10 feet away from the psi-wheel, and it started moving before I even got close to it. I even did it from a distance. It worked really well, and that surprised me. I did some research and saw that the wheel was susceptible to wind currents, so I turned off the fan on my computer and sealed off my windows and everything else, so there was nothing to stir the air. I was sure there was no wind blowing anywhere, and the wheel started spinning again when I tested it.

I always believed that I could move objects, I just never really thought of trying the psi-wheel thing. I have always believed in the paranormal; I've felt cold spots and ghosts and things from time to time in the places I lived that are supposedly haunted.

The strange thing about the psi-wheel experiments is that I take a little break when I do them because I get really, really hungry. It's the weirdest thing. I ate three meals that first night, and I don't usually eat more than two a day. I found myself craving vegetables more than anything else, and I wouldn't really believe what happened if it wasn't for the hungry part.

Maybe it's the life-energy of the plants that my system was seeking. I was talking to someone online who said there's a theory that telekinetic energy takes up some body mass. That might be interesting for some of your readers to research.

Brian
Pennsylvania

Chapter 60

Would You Like a Sweet?

This happened about 15 years ago. I was with my boy-friend at the time, and we both fell asleep. You know some-times when you fall asleep, you wake up with a sudden jerk? Well, that's what happened, with an added twist.

We both woke up at the same time, and it was weird because we both started to describe our dream. It wasn't like I described my dream and he said, "Yeah, that happened to me." We both started saying the exactly the same thing. Well, what happened to us both in the dream was that we were traveling in a car on the opposite side of the road, which meant that we weren't in England, where I'm originally from, but in a different country, and it was raining really, really hard. There was a child in the backseat. And when the child reached his hand out and offered a candy, that's when my boyfriend turned around and the car crashed. In the dream I knew my boyfriend and I were so romantic, we were living together in the future, and we were out in a foreign country, traveling.

Well, about a year later, we took a holiday to Orlando, Florida, and me being a nice big sister, we took my little brother with us. He was about 11 years old at the time. So we were driving in Florida with my little brother, and it was raining really, really hard. Some cars were even pulling over to the side of the road because they didn't want to be driving in the horrible weather. My little brother had a packet of Skittles and he reached his hand out and offered my boyfriend a sweet, and when he turned to take it...that's when we both realized, *no no no no!* Right there, on the road, we both remembered the dream we'd had about a year before about the kid in the back, the bad weather, and all of those details. It was really freaky.

When he put his hand through the opening between the seats with the packet of Skittles, and my boyfriend said, "Oh, have you got any purple ones?" then we were like, "Oh my God!" You know?

I absolutely believe that dream stopped us from getting into a terrible accident. The boyfriend didn't last, so it wasn't that romantic ideal that I had about him in the dream and our future together, but the details were all there. I think that dream prevented a tragedy.

Michelle

Minnesota

Chapter 61

The Tree With a Face

To set the stage, when this all happened I was in the U.S. Navy and I'd just changed religions from Christianity to Wicca. I was at a park nearby the port with another serviceman, and we were talking and hanging out when this strange incident occurred.

We were shooting the breeze, relaxing, talking about gaming, sci-fi, occult matters, and all that. Suddenly, I got a vibe that there was something on a tree. This unknown sensation. I asked him to get a flashlight. He said, "Sure." I asked him to shine the flashlight at this part of the tree where I got this weird instinct that something was there, and as he did we could see an image on the tree. It kind of looked like a face on the tree, and it looked like we had scared the crud out of it!

I think we actually scared the spirit because I don't think it expected us to know it was there. I think it was just sitting there, watching us.

I'm more sensitive to things like this, and when you open up your mind you kind of become open to more occurrences. I don't believe in everything supernatural, but I've had some strange, unexplained coincidences happen in my life.

We went back to that park later and shined the flashlight where I'd seen the face previously, and it just looked like the normal tree bark. We did not see that image ever again, not after that one night. When we saw it, the amazing thing was that the face looked like yours or mine—a human face on a tree!

Ryan
Florida

Chapter 62

Here Comes Peter Cottontail?

I was around 8 or 9 years old, and it was my weekend to be at my father's house. It was the weekend of Easter, so, Saturday night I was very excited and wouldn't go to sleep. I couldn't get to sleep, trying to stay awake for the Easter Bunny. As soon as I was about to doze off, I heard these three loud bumps, almost like knocks, downstairs. I thought it was my father playing a joke on us, you know? I looked over and saw my sister lying next to me and my father on his bed. There wasn't anybody else; everybody was where they were supposed to be. You would think there might be people milling about, "helping the Easter Bunny," as it were, but everybody was where they were supposed to be, and there wasn't anyone else in the house. I tried to go back to sleep, and it happened again: three loud noises. I couldn't explain it—and I'm getting goosebumps right now, oh my goodness.

This was back in the '80s, and I know the house was roughly 100 years old at the time, so I don't know if it was the pipes banging, or if it was my grandmother—I know she died in the house about 10 years before this. It's hard to explain exactly what it was.

After this happened my father ended up selling the house, and misfortune fell to the lady that bought it. I ended up reading in the newspaper that it burned down, and she didn't know why. They couldn't figure out what caused it to burn down. Maybe what I heard that night was more sinister than the Easter Bunny.

Karen
New York

Chapter 63

The Family Bible

The house that I grew up in with my five siblings and my mom and dad was in a quiet cul-de-sac, in a small city (back then), in Mequon, in 1972. You know how they say that kids pick up on things? Well, I guess as a kid I did not pick up on things, but my siblings did: things like footsteps and objects misplaced and then turning up. But I did experience a few strange things in the house. The first one was after my mom passed away, when I was about 12. My stepmother was in the house at the time, so it was my dad, my stepmother, and myself, and we'd just gone up to bed when there was this really loud thump on the living-room floor. It was a hardwood floor. My stepmother and I went downstairs to check it out. It was the family Bible, which had been in a built-in bookshelf, on the bottom shelf, probably only two inches up from the ground. If it had fallen out from that distance, it would not have made that loud noise. It seemed as though someone or something took it off of the shelf and slammed it on the floor.

This happened after my mom died, but I don't know that I necessarily tie the two together. It's just interesting because so many other weird things happened in the house.

When I was a little bit older, in high school, my parents went out of town. It was just my older brother and I alone in the house, so he'd had some friends over that night, and I had a friend stay overnight. We didn't have any full-blown house parties or anything like that; there were just a couple of people over. So after the three of us—my brother, my friend, and I—had gone on to bed, in the middle of the night my girlfriend and I sat up in bed, at the same time, and we heard a woman crying and a man consoling her. Like, in the middle of our living room.

It was very bizarre. And so we sat there and listened, and then we went downstairs to check it out, and there was no one there. There was no sign that anyone had been there. No footsteps. Nothing.

Well, we've talked about it in the years since we've lived there, since my parents sold the house. And we did learn that someone two doors down had shot themselves to death. Plus, I learned we were living on what had been Native American territory. That next morning after my girlfriend and I heard that woman crying and the man consoling her, there was a mysterious turquoise ring in the bathroom. There's an old story that there was a chief, Potawatomi, who had a daughter named Mequon, who ran off with her lover. I don't know; I don't know if that's a true story or not, but with that ring appearing from nowhere, it sure makes you think!

Kelly
Wisconsin

Chapter 64

Easy Rider on the Other Side

I've had a very explainable, predictable life. But there are two events in it that I just definitely cannot explain. They occurred while I lived in Wessington Springs, South Dakota, a small farm town in the middle of the state. I had a great childhood. I tell you, the people there are great, salt-of-the-earth-type people. If you were going through a tough time, I'd say, "How's it going, Jim?" and you'd say "Great, how about you?" That type of people just didn't share these kinds of stories.

The story I want to start with is about when I was driving my motorcycle out to a friend's farm, which is about two miles out on this paved and then gravel road. The gravel road had this ravine on the way, and if I went about 60 miles per hour across it, I'd feel a loss of gravity like the astronauts feel for about two seconds, and then I'd hit the road on the other side of the ravine. I tell you, when you're young, you're invincible. Although it was definitely fun, it was not smart. Well, that night, when it was time to go home, it was very dark and there was absolutely no moon in the sky. And when you're out in the country like that, there are definitely no lights. So the no-moon nights were black, like...well, it was really, really dark that night.

So, I took off, and I was heading down that gravel road and got up to my 60 miles per hour as I headed up to the ravine, and all of a sudden my bike just died. I mean, dead as dead. I had no lights, and I had to slow the bike down and stop it. I stopped just before the ravine, and I said to myself, *Man, I'm glad I didn't touch down in that ravine when that went out.*

I knew it was electrical, so I checked the levels on the battery and one other thing I knew it might be: the fuse. I couldn't see it, and I'd never changed one before, but I knew where it was. I knew I was going to have to push my bike back to the guy's farm and change the fuse under the farm lights. So, muttering—quite a bit—I pushed my bike the half a mile or more back to his farm, found the fuse, replaced it, and then started my bike again and took off. And I knew that was my last fuse, so I said to myself, *I don't know what caused the first one to go out, so I'm going to take it nice and slow and worry about this later.* So I was going, now, 15 to 20 miles per hour, and I got to that ravine. I headed down to the ravine at 15 miles per hour, and suddenly I locked on my brakes and stopped. And I tell you what, when people say the hair on your neck and arms stands up, I know exactly what that means.

Right in front of me was a herd of cows that had gotten loose. And I tell you, if I had flown into that ravine at 60 miles per hour like I did the first time, I'd have gone right into the herd, and I'm sure that I would have killed myself. I've never had a blown fuse before on that bike, or after with that bike, or on any other bike. I'm telling you, if that bike had not died at the right time that night, I believe I would have died.

Taking a different approach, when bad things happen to me I always think, *Well, maybe it happened for a reason.* So, it's changed the way I look at life sometimes.

I also have another motorcycle-related unexplainable event to relate—and don't worry, when I got married I sold my bikes, to my wife's relief. This story I've shared with only one other person in my life, and that's because I'm still scared by it. I couldn't tell my family; my dad was a doctor, and my mom was against me buying a motorcycle because she was sure I'd kill myself. Little did she know. It reminded me of *A Christmas Story*: Remember when Santa Claus says, "You're going to shoot your eyes out with that BB gun"? Well, that's the same reason I couldn't tell my mom, because if I had ever told her this story, she would have taken away my bike and I'd be riding my tricycle still today.

Well, I was riding in the gully area of Wessington Springs, and I went into an area where there were a lot of trees, and I went to duck underneath a branch, but I'd forgotten about that added height of the helmet, and wham! I was knocked off my bike and to the ground, on my back. As I lay there I heard my bike keep going for a little bit, tip over, and eventually I heard it die.

I tried to get up, and I could not move anything on my body. I mean, nothing was moving. So I tried to speak, and I couldn't even speak, so I knew I was severely hurt, and thought I probably broke my neck. But the thing was, I felt absolutely no pain. And then I heard this dog behind me start barking. He was right behind my head area. I could hear this—and I was very happy to hear it, and I'll tell you why: I thought someone must be around with their dog. Well, there were six people, men and women in their upper 60s to 70s in age, dressed in '50s-era clothing (which is not unusual for my hometown anyways, even today) coming into sight, and they were leaning over me. Some were standing over me, and I still couldn't move or talk. As soon as they came into view, the dog behind me stopped barking. I never did see the dog. Now, when I saw them, they weren't like ghostly apparition-type things; they were clearly visible, but I could also see the trees and the sky, and these people had like a different tint to them. But they were clearly identifiable, and the one thing that was very unusual for me was—because in a small town you know everyone; sometimes more than you want to—I didn't recognize a single one of them!

The first thing that came to mind was, *I've died, I'm in heaven, and heaven is just filled with old people. Like*

Florida! I tell you what, man, I was really disappointed, because I was 16 at the time, and I thought, *Oh, this is Heaven.* And so I lay there, and this one old man knelt down and he was right over my face, and he was studying me. But no one ever touched me, and no one ever talked directly to me. He looked very concerned, and he was talking to the other people, and they were all talking amongst themselves, and they were all worried about me. And the old man said that it was my neck and I was hurt really bad. And the conversations, like I said, weren't really *to* me; they were debating, and some of them were saying, "Oh, he's going to be okay," and the others were saying, "No, he's hurt really bad. He's not going to be okay." And I'm thinking, *Well, go get help. Do something. Don't just stand there talking about it.* And I tell you, Jim, clear as a bell, I could identify these people today. Their faces are very clear to me as I'm talking today.

And, well, there was one point when the old man reached some sort of conclusion, because he said, "Yep," and he stood up and he walked out of my view, and then each person sort of started walking off. And I remember the last old lady, she gave me just the saddest look, before she also went out of my sight. At that sad look, I got the feeling I was going to die, and that really bothered me. I wondered why they left me there, because they knew I was hurt, and it didn't seem to me that they were going to get help, and as soon as they were out of sight, the dog started barking again. In the same spot behind me.

I thought, *Oh my God, they left their dog there.* It was a little confusing to me, and I don't know how long I was there, but I started eventually to be able to move my toes, and then I started moving my fingers, and then I moved my ankles. I didn't want to push anything, because I sincerely thought my neck was broken. Eventually I was able to move my legs, and then I thought, *Okay, I'm going to try to sit up*, and I sat up, and eventually I stood up and I started moving my neck. My voice didn't come back; I still couldn't talk.

I know I had hit my head hard, and maybe it was all that, but I do remember hearing my bike continue on when I hit the ground, and then I heard it tip over. So I was conscious for that. Then I heard it stop running. I know that I had no pain, and that I was conscious.

Here's the part that still scares me today: I got up, and turned to look where that dog was barking, exactly where I heard that dog barking, and I saw a horrible sight, Jim, horrible. In the exact spot where I heard the dog barking, there, chained to a tree, was the corpse of a dog that had been there at least two weeks. It was a horrible death, Jim. I'm telling you, somebody cruelly chained this dog to a tree, and I could see the circular pattern the dog had made. It probably died of thirst. It was so horrible, I got over to my bike, and I got out of there. I was so scared by that, the whole mess, that I went straight to my home, and into my room, and I didn't go out until—I was hoping my voice would come back. After about two hours of being home my voice came back. So I knew I didn't have to tell anybody this one; I think I got a break.

About two days later, Jim, I went back to that spot, and I looked at that tree branch, and I saw the dog's corpse again, and I said a little prayer for the dog. I had to go back there to make sure that I'd seen it, and it was true. I tell you, I'll never go back to that spot again in my life.

I haven't researched the town since then. But they do have a museum now, in that town, and that's a great idea. I could go back and probably do some research, and I'm telling you I'd recognize the people I saw in a heartbeat.

I know that dog was barking from that spot...I don't know about dog ghosts, but I do feel strongly that, for whatever reason, that dog was barking. And I don't know, it's just my gut feeling, but I feel those people were there for that dog for some reason, and then my issue took place. I don't know if they had any input on my being able to get up and walk again, because I've never suffered any critical problems since then. I have no clue, and that's why I'll say that it was one of the two unexplainable events in my life. I will tell you, it still scares me today.

Mark

Minnesota

Chapter 65

What Are the Chances?

I had some good friends who moved to the southwest of England, down in Cornwall, and they invited me to go and stay with them for a bit. Eventually I got everything synchronized and I went down to see them. One of my friends said, "Well, we're going to take you out to an old smugglers' pub in Cornwall in Falmouth, and we're going to meet up with some friends that have just come back from holiday."

I said, "Oh, that would be nice." So we went down to this old pub, and it's a real old one. It went back...gosh, centuries. Really great atmosphere. My friends went to the bar to get some drinks, and I was left with their friends, and it can be a bit difficult to strike up conversation. I remembered that I'd been told that they'd just come back from holiday, so my first opener to them was, "Oh, did you have a good holiday?" They said, "Oh, yeah, really marvelous." I said, "Where did you go?" They said, "We stayed in England; we went to see some friends and stay at their house in

Hampshire." I said, "Oh, that's interesting. That's where I grew up. Whereabouts was it?" They said, "We were in a little village near a town called Petersfield." I said, "That's pretty much where I grew up. What was the name of the village?" And they said, "It was a very small place called Liss." I said, "Well, that's a big coincidence; that's the exact village where I grew up as a boy, and spent most of my formative years."

I said, "Just out of interest, whereabouts were you staying?" They said, "Well, you go out of the railway station and head out of the village along such-and-such road, and it was up there somewhere."

Now my interest was really piqued, so I continued my query. "Well, that's more interesting," I said, "because that's pretty much the area where I lived as a boy. So whereabouts was it then?" They said, "Well, it's a place on Rake Road," and I said, "That's pretty much where my parents' house was; which house was it?" They said, "Well, it's an old place called Thorn Cottage, set back off the road. Big old white house." I said, "Well, that's my old house!"

I'd never met these people before. This is where it started to get spooky. I said, "Well, just out of interest, which room did you stay in?" They said, "Well, you go through the door, up the staircase, turn right from the staircase, and we were in that room." I said, "I don't believe this; that's my old room." And I started to feel the hair on the back of my neck stand up. They slept in my old room!

This business about synchronicity that I've heard people talk about, it's just...you couldn't plan it, could you? It just happens, and when it does, it knocks you sideways. Like I say, these people couldn't have known all these facts about me.

Even my friends wouldn't have known—the people that invited me to stay—they just couldn't have known the details. But that's the way it happened. My friends were obviously amazed, because these people were very close friends of theirs, and they just couldn't believe that it all fell into place the way it did. It just got spookier as the whole thing got around, because I was thinking, *I don't believe this. I really don't.* I felt I was being set up, but when I questioned them, "This isn't a setup, is it?" They were adamant it wasn't.

Tim

United Kingdom

Chapter 66

A Cold Blast on a Hot August Night

My mother and I were coming home from the movies at about 10 o'clock in the evening. It was one of those August nights when it was still really horrible out even though it was late. We were just walking past this spot we'd walked past a million times because it's on the way to school, to the supermarket, to church, et cetera. We would literally walk past this spot six to eight times a day. This one night we were walking past and it was really hot and muggy and we both got a blast of cold air that made us stop dead in our tracks. We just looked at each other and said, "What the heck is that?" There were the railroad tracks elevated on an embankment on our right, an office building that was closed a few houses down the block, and nothing else. We couldn't figure out where the cold air was coming from, and then we noticed it was in a very confined space; you could wrap your arms around it like a column of cold air, straight up, straight down.

Here we were in the 1970s like two crazy people with our arms out trying to get the circumference, the height, and how far the cold spot went down. We walked over to the building across the street to see if their air conditioner was on. The houses down the block were quiet and there were no air conditioners running. We could not figure out where it was coming from.

Well, that particular spot was the site of one of the Long Island Rail Road's worst train wrecks, back in the 1950s—1950 Thanksgiving evening, I believe it was. There were 79 people killed when one train rammed into another. This cold spot was in that stretch of track. I went to try to research it to see exactly where, and it was between Jamaica Station and Kew Gardens, where there was a Richmond Hill stop that is no longer there. I believe it was closed because of that accident. And there were a number of railroad cars involved so the accident area kind of spread from where we were down to the point of collision. So the wreck was in that area; that's the only thing I could think of causing the cold spot. I never heard anything weird about it. The only thing people would say was, "Oh yeah, back in the '50s it was that really bad train wreck." It was just such an oddity!

Jean
New York

Part V: Eating My Own Dogfood

At the beginning of this book, I mentioned that I have felt destined to be involved in the paranormal world. This feeling did not come only from my childhood fascination with programs like *In Search Of* or *The Twilight Zone*, but something far more personal. Experiences of my own and of loved ones have convinced me that there is something to all of these paranormal stories.

My family is salt-of-the-earth, and certainly not the type to sleep with crystals under their beds to summon some universal wisdom or study their chakras. To them, a cigar is a cigar, and life is pretty straightforward. Yet, I grew up with supernatural stories and later experienced my own weird tales that solidified my lifelong obsession with the topic at hand.

So, join me as I close this book by telling my own stories and "eating my own dogfood" around the CAMPFIRE.

Chapter 67

It Lit Up the Whole Sky

Chapters 67 and 68 are stories that my father has told me since I was a small child. I'm always fascinated by them.

One night at about 11 o'clock we were back in the mountains on vacation and me and your mom decided to take a ride through the mountains, and we pulled off and went up an old log road and we stopped in there. We stopped for a while and I had a bottle of beer—which I know I shouldn't have been doing—and it was pitch dark. (This was 40 years ago, so I don't think the law is going to come after me.) You could hardly see anything. It was pitch dark. We were sittin' there talkin' and all of a sudden there was a light so bright, when it lit up, it lit the whole car up on the inside and everything around it. You could see the minute-hand on the clock in the car, it was so bright. It only lasted for about three seconds. You could see the background of the trees and everything; the side of the hills; everything. But it didn't last long.

I looked out the side window and it seemed like there was a person standing there. He looked to be, maybe, shoulder-length to the glass in the side of the door. He looked like he had some sort of a welding mask on.

Well, something was standing there, but I turned to your mom and told her to look and when we turned around it was gone. Well, it kind of scared me so we got out of there. I drove out and went down and went on the other road and started out of there. There were all kinds of birds, four or five of them, up along the bank. The funny thing was that they were the biggest birds I've ever seen. I had never seen anything like it.

They were just really big birds; they had a wingspan of...I don't know how big they were, but boy, you could see them. I think there were about four of them. Then about every 50 feet or 100 feet you could see one or two up along the bank. That's what I saw. Your mom saw it too, but your mom didn't see the person standing there beside the car. This was back up in the mountains where there was no traffic or anything. I thought, *Well, tomorrow you'll hear somebody say they saw a light*, but I never did hear any more about it.

I never did believe in things like that, but when I see something with my own eyes, then I believe it. And your mom was there, too, and I asked her, "What do you think that was?" She said, "I have no idea at all." We never did take another ride out there after that. Not at night, anyway. It's right up there in the mountains; it's all mountains. It's all wilderness. I never did see anything like that again; that was the only time. Yeah, it scared me a little bit.

Jim Harold, Sr.

Chapter 68

There's Someone in Here

Me and my brother worked in the steel mill together. This must have been the late '50s or early '60s. We had been workin' the 3-to-11 shift, and we came home to our apartment over a bar in the city. Well, we came home and we ate something, we watched television a little bit, and then we went to bed.

About 3 o'clock in the morning, something woke me up, I don't know what it was. I was lying on my side, and when I rolled over, this old fella was standing there above me. I remembered the guy: He used to come in the bar there all the time and I used to talk to him, get him a few drinks, ya know?

He must've been up in his 80s. Anyway, one time I was in there I asked the fella that owned it, "What happened to the old fella that used to come in here?" He said, "Well, he passed away." I never thought anything more about it.

Well, here was that guy over my bed about half a year after that. When I woke up, it scared me and I kind of swung at it, and nothin' was there but air. I hollered real loud for my brother. He got up out of bed and came around and he said, "Aww, you're having a nightmare."

I should say it was in the summertime so the windows were open because it was real hot, but our apartment was up about three stories. So nobody could've come through a window. Me and my brother, we started checking all around the apartment. All the doors were locked and there was only one window open—nobody could've gotten in there.

Well, he said "You're having a nightmare; you should forget it." So I went back to sleep and didn't think any more about it. And about two weeks later, in the middle of the night, I heard my brother holler. So I jumped up and he told me, he said, "Jim, there's somebody in here." And we checked all around and he described the old guy to me and I said, "Well, that's the same one I saw in here." He didn't think it was a nightmare then!

We stayed there two or three years after that, and we never did ever see anything else. I know it wasn't a dream. I never believed in ghosts, but when I see one with my own eyes, then I believe it because I've seen it.

Jim Harold, Sr.

Chapter 69

AK-47s Can Make You a Believer

This first-person account of mine is not "paranormal," per se, but, similar to the upcoming "Why I Hate Logging Trucks" chapter, it makes me ponder questions of coincidence, fate, and destiny. Are some things meant to be, while others aren't? You be the judge.

It was the summer of 1994, and I was very much in love with my new girlfriend, Dar—still am, in fact. She has been my wife for the last 14 years, and I am blessed. Though we are thankfully still very into each other, that summer was a special time for us—a time without a mortgage, kids, or many adult responsibilities. Most of you know that thrill when you first start going out with someone. That person is perfect! Every minute is a revelation, and every experience is accentuated. So, we were having a great time...one of the best of my life.

All that week, we were looking forward to the weekend. Every weekend was a party for us. We weren't particularly wild; our average weekend entailed seeing a movie or going out drinking a bit with our friends. In short, it was a heck of a lot of fun. This weekend was going to be even better than usual: Thanks to my menial job at a local radio station, we got free tickets to one of the best amusement parks in the country, Cedar Point. We were going to go with a couple of friends and their family. We were jazzed about it.

At 24, I was still a kid in many ways. I loved roller coasters and amusement parks. The trip would also be a chance to get out of my house, which I hated. I grew up in the Broadway area of Cleveland, in the city. Once a proud, working-class area, it had fallen into ruin. About eight months before this story begins, I had moved to a Slavic Village home that was considered a slight move up from where I'd grown up. It was an old, two-story, A-frame house, dark blue in color. I wasn't crazy about it. It was too much house for me; I didn't have the furniture to fill it—I was making slave wages at the station—and it seemed unsafe. Next door, there seemed to be a bunch of unsupervised teenagers who had taken up residence. I had told Dar my concerns, and she said I was being paranoid. But, I had this feeling...

In fact, I had just signed a lease for a modest apartment in the suburbs where—guess what—Dar lived. But it wouldn't be ready for a few weeks, so I was stuck in Slavic Village. I had told my landlord that week that I would be moving soon. I don't think he was thrilled with it, but he was a very good guy. He liked me because I didn't have crazy parties or tear up his place, and I paid my rent on time like clockwork.

Back to Cedar Point: We went that Saturday and had the great time we had predicted. Little did I know as were driving home that it could have been my *last* good time—or my last time experiencing anything at all on this earth, if things had worked out slightly differently...

My friends had driven us all because they had a mini-van, and they dropped Dar and me at my place at about 1:30 a.m. to pick up my car so I could drive her home, about 40 minutes away. All the way there, she insisted that I ask her father, Antonio, if I could sleep on their couch overnight. She was very concerned that I would fall asleep driving back to my place. She was right; I was exhausted, but I was very reluctant to stay. Her father scared the hell out of me. He was an Italian-born working-class guy and not exactly what you'd call "warm and fuzzy." Don't get me wrong, he was always nice to me, but I could see that he would probably not be so nice if you crossed him. At that point, Dar and I had only been going out for about four months, and I didn't feel that I was in a position to ask to sleep over. In fact, I was dead set against it.

Still, after about 30 minutes of jawboning, I gave in. I slept over, there were no problems, and we all actually had a nice family breakfast the next morning. At that point, I could tell that I had been accepted by her father. Dar later told me that her dad would never have done that for anyone else she'd dated. It was a high compliment.

I drove home that Sunday, feeling happy. Feeling good about pretty much everything. Even though it had been only four months, I could see that Dar and I had a long-term future. I drove up to my house and parked on the street, right in front of my erstwhile abode.

Across the street, I saw Dave, the landlord's son. He was talking to a neighbor and pointing toward our side of the street. I walked over to see what was up.

"Hi Dave, what's going on?" I asked innocently—I was very green. "We've got to talk," he said, "there's been a drive-by."

Still clueless, I asked him whose house had been hit. "Our house," he said.

Upon further examination while we walked over to the wounded two-story, I could see holes in the windows and the wooden siding.

In 1994, this was certainly a "changing" neighborhood, but still considered one of the city's safer areas. Several years later, it would really start a downhill slide, but not yet. Not in 1994.

It turns out that several rounds of armor-piercing AK-47 fire had been launched into our home sometime in the early morning hours, while I was peacefully sleeping on Antonio's couch. Talking to Dave, I could tell that he was shaken. He lived in the back of the house and slept on the first floor, and live rounds had flown around him when all of this went down.

I went into my apartment and was astonished at the sight. The double-door fridge that my uncle had given me had a hole in both exterior walls and the internal one, too. A ketchup bottle inside had taken a direct hit. My poor microwave, which I'd only had for a couple of months, had been used for target practice, and didn't stand a chance. I always slept on the second floor, and no rounds had landed there, but if I'd been there, could these would-be assassins have been lying in wait for me? Would I have gotten thirsty in the middle of the night, and ventured into to the firing zone for a drink of water? Who knows?

According to the landlord's son, the police who came to investigate were astonished that such a violent act had taken place in this relatively peaceful neighborhood. So, they wanted to know more about me...I guess they initially thought I might be some kind of underworld kingpin or drug dealer. If you knew me personally, you'd realize how truly hilarious that is! I laugh even now thinking about it.

Later that day, with the help of my friend who had gone with us to Cedar Point, I got all of my belongings out of my house and into his garage. I never stayed another night in what had become a modern-day O.K. Corral. Because my apartment wouldn't be ready for another month, I stayed in Antonio's spare room—I must really have passed the test!

But why was my house shot up? Remember those un-supervised teenagers next door? Well, my dear Dar was wrong. I wasn't being paranoid; I was being observant. Having lived in the city for 23 years must have given me some street smarts. The kids were no good—and, worse, they lived in a light-blue house next to my dark-blue one. It seems they had been involved in the theft of some motorcycle parts. I made myself scarce after the shooting happened, so I don't have many details, but they may have crossed a gang of some type. Bad move.

Luckily for the teenagers next door, at the time of the shooting, it was dark, and the street lights lent an orange tint to everything. So, when the shooters were told to hit a blue house on our block, their light-blue house looked white, whereas mine looked very blue—bang bang: dead fridge and microwave.

As I said at the beginning, this story is not paranormal, per se. However, it is one hell of a coincidence. Would I have been killed if I had been there that night? Maybe.

A great marriage and two kids later, I often think of that night, and how things could have been different. So, when somebody asks me if I believe in fate I say, "There's a good shot there's something to it!"

Jim Harold

Chapter 70

Why I Hate Logging Trucks

While visiting my cousin in West Virginia in the late '80s, I had an experience that I'll never forget. It was really weird, and potentially fatal.

One of the things I loved to do in West Virginia was walk around and experience the majestic beauty of Mother Nature. Though my family was from the sticks, I was born and bred in the inner city. Not the suburbs, but the cold, hard city. Growing up I could see the smokestacks of the steel mills of Republic Steel from my house. So getting to breathe the fresh air was quite a treat.

After a few days of my expeditions, I heard through the grapevine (my cousin) that one of the neighbor girls liked the cut of my jib. [Author's note: I was pretty cute back then.]

Anyhow, I was leaving later this particular day to go back to the big city, but somehow the neighbor girl and I had arranged to meet through my cousin. Our big rendezvous was a 15-minute walk through the small town. I can't imagine what we thought would come of it; this was pre-Internet so no Skyping here.

After talking and walking, we came up to a large logging truck parked on the side of the road. We split up, and each of us walked on one side of the truck with a huge load of chained logs, she on the left and I on the right. As I walked past it, something told me to get the hell away from that truck. I had the sense that those logs were going to fall off. I walked past the truck a little faster than I would normally have, and chalked the feeling up to my overactive imagination.

We walked about another 15 feet and then we heard a loud noise behind us. Sure enough, the logs had fallen off exactly where I had been walking. I wasn't so paranoid after all. The girl and I walked a little more, and exchanged addresses. I don't think we ever communicated after that. I think were were both so freaked out we just decided to drop it then and there.

So, Christine, wherever you are, I hope it's been a nice life so far. Continued best wishes. And one more thing: Stay away from those damned logging trucks.

Jim Harold

Chapter 77

Turn Your Radio On

For those not familiar, "Turn Your Radio On" is the title of an old country gospel song.

About a dozen years ago, I had an experience involving my radio. It did not pick up God, as the song suggests, but I am pretty sure that it picked up a signal from my brother, who had died just a few days before.

My brother, Hughie, was autistic. I've mentioned it on my shows a few times. My parents were devoted to my brother and were determined not to "lock him away in a home." This I admire; their self-sacrifice was unbelievable. But I do think that they made him so dependent on them that they were actually hurting him, making him less self-sufficient than he could have been. That being said, now, as a parent of two young girls, I have no idea how I would have reacted to such a burden. It was an incredibly tough situation.

My parents had moved to a rural area down south as I stayed in Ohio after college. I got married and bought a home, so I was staying put up north. I would generally visit them a couple times a year. We talked on a regular basis, so I was always up-to-date on everyone's health. Early in one particular week in February, my mom told me that they had taken my brother to the doctor because he had a very nasty cold. Three or four days later, I called and spoke to him. He could only speak in somewhat unintelligible words, but my mom put him on the line, I said hello, and he grunted "Hi" back.

I could tell that he was very congested, and I expressed my concern. The next day at work, I worried about him and had a really ominous feeling. That night at about 10 p.m., my uncle called and said that they had taken Hughie to the nearest hospital about 20 miles away. He had been rushed there by an ambulance. He was having trouble breathing, so my parents acted quickly.

After the call, I told my wife, Dar, that I thought my brother was going to die. She thought I was overreacting.

He was still in his 20s, and there was no reason to think the doctors couldn't stabilize him at the hospital. But I was so worried that I stayed up until about 2 a.m. to hear what happened. When I got the call, I found out that, sadly, I was right. He had died from severe pneumonia. I was shocked; it seemed so surreal—impossible. *That poor boy, to be born with autism and now—this.*

Dar, pregnant with our first daughter, and I packed up the next day and took the unenviable trip. It was horrible. My parents had so wrapped their lives around Hughie that it was as though their reason for being had evaporated. They might not like that I am writing this chapter. They have never gotten over Hughie's death; my brother's room is almost exactly the way it was when he died—more than a decade ago.

The trip back home was tough. We talked about what had happened as I scanned around the radio and found a "Music of Your Life" station. I have always liked these stations because I love the music of Sinatra, Nat King Cole, and the like. Anyhow, taking a little comfort from the radio was something to draw my attention away from the terrible experience of the last week.

My brother had liked music, too. He loved different kinds. Of all people, he really liked Lawrence Welk. When we were little kids in the '70s, Welk's show was still in syndication and Hughie had taken quite a liking to it. Once the show went over to PBS he continued to watch it; it was a favorite. This was unusual for a 20-something, but Hughie's condition made him different from the average bear. It was fair to say that he thought Welk was "wunerful, wunerful," as Welk used to say on his shows. He was probably one of Hughie's top three or four favorite musicians.

Anyhow, as I was talking to Dar in the car, I noticed this instrumental playing on the radio. The song sounded familiar but because it had no words, I couldn't figure it out. After it was over, the DJ about made me run off the road. "That, of course, was Lawrence Welk with his 1961 hit, 'Calcutta,'" said the announcer.

You have to remember that, even in the late '90s, you did not hear Lawrence Welk on the radio, not even on an oldies station. It was highly unusual for that rather obscure cut to be played—and at the exact time we were driving in that area, on the exact station I'd turned to? I am convinced that Hughie was saying, somehow, "I'm alright, big brother, don't worry about me. It's okay."

Somehow, he managed to communicate from the other side better than he could have when he was living with autism. I'm so glad I turned my radio on that day and heard his transmission. Here's mine if you're listening, Hughie. I love you, brother.

Jim Harold

Herman

by Campfire Essay Contest Winner
Janese

We thought that it would be fun to have a "Campfire Essay Contest" in which listeners could submit their stories of strangeness. Thanks to all of our entrants! Congratulations to Janese Fundock for her winning entry: "Herman."

I am no stranger to the paranormal. My mother's farmhouse, a few miles away from my grandparents', is nearly 200 years old, and we have had many paranormal experiences there—everything from levitating objects to disappearing/reappearing objects, cold spots, footsteps, music that has no source, and full-body apparitions. All of these and more became routine growing up on the farm. The paranormal doesn't shake me, but it does make me more interested to find out the truth.

About eight years ago, I had an experience I'll never forget. I was 22 years old, a military wife, and a new mother. My husband was deployed overseas, so my 11-month-old daughter and I were living with my grandparents. Both of my grandparents were in failing health. The house was only about 50 years old, having been built by my grandfather in the 1960s. My daughter and I shared a bedroom in the finished basement of the house.

One clear summer night, I was lying in bed, not yet asleep. My daughter was in her crib a few feet from my bed. The top three feet or so of the basement where we were staying was above ground, with windows high up on the walls allowing the moonlight to shine in the room. The windows were open; it was a warm night that is typical for early summer in the Pennsylvania countryside.

Suddenly, I became aware of a very uncomfortable feeling. I couldn't quite establish what this feeling was, just that I was feeling very, very uneasy. I glanced down toward the bottom of the bed and saw what I thought was my daughter toddling along the bottom of the bed. I could only see the shadow of the top of her head and I remember thinking that she must have crawled out of her crib and was coming to get in bed with me. I smiled and laid my head back down, waiting for her to come to the side of the bed. I felt her grab the bedspread to pull herself up on top of the bed, and I thought I would give her a little help. When I tried to reach over to the side of the bed, though, I found I was unable to move. My first reaction was that this was very strange. The seconds passed, and I still couldn't move. I could feel her tugging on the bedcovers, climbing up the side, and I became alarmed, thinking I was having a stroke or seizure...

any explanation for my sudden paralysis. Just then, the little figure made it up on top of the bed and crawled over to me, and I fought a panic I've never felt before. It was not my daughter. It was not human at all. I don't know what exactly it was, but it was roughly two feet tall, greenish-brown, and resembled what I can only describe as "Yoda." I was in a full-blown panic; I could feel my heart pounding and my chest heaving and I was shaking like a leaf. This thing crawled up onto my chest and sat down, cross-legged, and just studied my face. I still couldn't move, and couldn't make a sound. I remember feeling my heart beating harder and harder. My breath was coming faster and faster, and I began to think that, if this continued, I was going to go into cardiac arrest. I have no idea how long it sat on me, just looking at me with a quizzical expression—30 seconds, maybe a few minutes—but it felt like an eternity.

Just when I thought that my heart was going to hammer right out of my chest, the little figure got a sudden look of complete surprise on his face. It never sad a word, but I distinctly felt it send a wave of emotion over me. It was as if it was telepathically apologizing for frightening me to such a degree, because it didn't mean to scare me. With that, it hopped up, jumped off the bed, and scampered out the door of the bedroom. Instantly I could move, and I flew out of bed. I grabbed my still-sleeping daughter out of her crib and ran with everything I had out through the apartment and up the stairs to the main house, flipping on every light I passed.

I spent the night in the recliner upstairs that night with the lights on, my daughter curled happily in my arms. For the next six months, I slept with all the lights blazing in the apartment at night. Then I figured if I gave it a silly, non-threatening name, I could make it a little less scary. So each night before bed, I would stop at my bedroom door, look around the apartment, and say, "No visits tonight, Herman." It helped...a little.

I still don't know what it was. It's never returned, and for that, I'm glad. I have never experienced anything like it before or since. I have been through some pretty distressing situations in my life, but I've never been so afraid of anything.

Janese
Pennsylvania

Lucifer In The Lamp

Jim's Pick: Campfire's Spookiest Story

I wanted to end the book with a story that you'd soon not forget. There have been so many spooky stories on the Campfire that is hard to pick one as the most spine tingling. This one gets my vote and, after all, it is my book so here it is!

I was about fifteen and my friend Bridget and I were looking for something to do after school one day, and she suggested a Ouija board that she had at home. So she pulled it out and we set it up on the floor. In order to make it a little more spooky, I guess, she turned off all the lights and just had a lava lamp for our light. It was set right next to the board.

She started asking questions like, "Is anyone there?" and it seemed to be responding and she asked for it to give us a sign. We waited. Nothing happened for awhile, so we moved on, and she kept asking other questions, and out of the corner of my eye I noticed the lava lamp. All of the wax was collecting in one solid ball, which I thought was weird. So I kept watching it, and slowly it was forming into the shape of something; so I pointed it out to my friend thinking that this was our sign. As we watched, it shaped into the form of the head of a devil and it was so detailed, and there's no way that a lava lamp could have made that much detail. It's mouth was open like it was growling, it had fangs, its eyes were very angry. It was facing us; it didn't move within the water of the lava lamp at all, it faced us the whole time, and then I said to my friend, "Oh my God, it's the devil" and we both took our hands off the board immediately and it just went back to the lava lamp bubbles.

After that, I didn't play with the board much. I tried it one other time with a different friend and I made sure every light in the house was on and the windows were open, thinking the dark maybe had something to do with it.

I don't know if it was evil necessarily, because it went away and it wasn't threatening. Maybe it was something playing a joke on us, a spirit...I don't know. I think it was something, and it definitely peaked my curiosity. I'm very fascinated with the paranormal, Ouija boards, Tarot cards, all those things. I think something had to have made that lava lamp do that.

LeAnn
Utah

Closing Thoughts

Thanks for reading *Jim Harold's Campfire: True Ghost Stories*. I appreciate it—as does my publisher! I hope to meet you again soon in the pages of my next book. Stay tuned.

Until then, we can stay in touch. Please take a listen to the podcast that inspired this book, JIM HAROLD'S CAMPFIRE. At my Website, *www.jimharold.com*, you can sign up to share your own stories on the show. If you are into the paranormal, please check out THE PARANORMAL PODCAST and my video podcast, THE PARANORMAL REPORT. You can find them all at jimharold.com and on iTunes. (For you non-techies, a podcast is really just an Internet radio show—you can listen right at my Website; its easy.) Enjoy! You can also e-mail me at jim@jimharold.com

I'd like to close with a little bit of wisdom gained from my fabulous audience: It is good to share your stories with someone—anyone. Whether it is with your families, with your friends, or on a radio show, please share. Our stories are our immortality, and we live on when we pass them along to the next generation.

Until we meet again, may all your stories have happy endings.

God Bless,
Jim Harold
April 25, 2011

Paranormal Resources on the Web

Here are some Websites that you might find interesting from the world of the paranormal.

astrologybymaria.com

bradandsherry.com

coasttocoastam.com

earthfiles.com

forteantimes.com

ghostvillage.com

jimharold.com (my personal favorite!)

jimharold.net (my membership site for even more content)

mufon.com

paranormal.about.com

paranormalnews.com

the-atlantic-paranormal-society.com

theastralworld.com

 251

Index

About the Author

Jim Harold has worked in radio, video, and business-to-business media. He holds a Master's degree in Applied Communication Theory and Methodology and has taught upper-level media business studies at a state university.

In 2005, Jim Harold created THE PARANORMAL PODCAST, an Internet radio show dedicated to all things supernatural. After more than a decade of working on the business side of media, Jim decided it was time to dust off his broadcasting skills and step back behind the mic. A lifelong interest in the paranormal, combined with his love of broadcasting and technology, resulted in the most successful podcast of its type to date. To his surprise and delight, Jim has become America's most popular paranormal podcaster.

He added a new podcast, JIM HAROLD'S CAMPFIRE, in 2009, and a video podcast, THE PARANORMAL REPORT in 2010. THE PARANORMAL PODCAST, JIM HAROLD'S CAMPFIRE, and THE PARANORMAL REPORT WITH CLAYTON MORRIS AND JIM HAROLD are each among the top podcasts in their categories on iTunes, often outranking programs from mainstream media publishers such as *The New York Times*, PBS, and NPR.

Jim lives in Ohio with his fantastic wife and two daughters. He is incredibly thankful for them and his loyal audience.

Jim won't dress up in alien costumes and doesn't plan on buying that $19.99 Super Official Ghost Detector off of late-night TV, but believes there is more to life than what meets the eye.

Jim Harold's Campfire: True Ghost Stories is his first book.